Figural
NODDERS

Identification & Value Guide

Hilma R. Irtz

COLLECTOR BOOKS
A Division of Schroeder Publishing Co., Inc.

The current values in this book should be used only as a guide. They are not intended to set prices, which vary from one section of the country to another. Auction prices as well as dealer prices vary greatly and are affected by condition as well as demand. Neither the Author nor the Publisher assumes responsibility for any losses that might be incurred as a result of consulting this guide.

Searching For A Publisher?

We are always looking for knowledgeable people considered to be experts within their fields. If you feel that there is a real need for a book on your collectible subject and have a large comprehensive collection contact Collector Books.

Cover Design: Karen Geary
Book Design: Kent Henry

On the cover

Top left: Japanese elder, pouring his sake. Nods yes. $450.00.
Top right: Campbell kid cookie jar. Neck spring. $75.00 – 100.00.
Center: Dachshund puppy head-hangers. Large $60.00. Small $45.00.
Bottom left: "Our Darling" swayer. Schäter & Vater. $225.00.
Bottom right: Granny and Grandpa harnessed their pigs for a joy ride. $475.00.

Additional copies of this book may be ordered from:

COLLECTOR BOOKS
P.O. Box 3009
Paducah, Kentucky 42002–3009

$19.95. Add $2.00 for postage and handling.

Copyright: Hilma R. Irtz, 1997

Printed in the U.S.A. by Image Graphics

Contents

Dedication

In loving memory, this book is dedicated to my late husband, *Frederick George Irtz.*

Acknowledgments

With grateful appreciation to my family and many friends who have encouraged and contributed to the successful completion of this book.

Dorothy Anthony

Vera Christy

Stanley C. Doerting

Shelley and Walter B. Ferguson

Bill and Mary Furnish

Frederick G. Irtz, II

Theodore W. Irtz

Iva Mae Long

Elaine Irtz Metzger

Rose and Henry Naetzger, Jr.

Marty and Ted Quell

Betsy Strisower

Betsy Zalewski

Photography credits

Bernadine & Harvey Abdon

Shelley Ferguson

Henry Naetzger, Jr.

Betsy Zalewski

The Author

Introduction

There is purpose for everything. My purpose is threefold.

Reason number one, a book on this subject has not been published and information from libraries and bookstores is unavailable. Therefore collectors and dealers ask and want to know.

My second reason goes back a number of years. It stems from my fascination with a small nodding figurine in an antique shop. I purchased it and brought it home. My curiosity was aroused and I wanted to know more, but information was nowhere to be found. Because research was so limited I began compiling my own data. This was the beginning of a learning experience. In time as I visited with other collectors, shop owners, and dealers, they were no more knowledgeable that I was. Countless times they said, "We need a book and some guidelines. Why don't *you* write one?"

My third reason was advanced through the support of my late husband, Frederick George Irtz. He was an inspiration and I am grateful for his confidence and understanding of my frustrations. My son, Frederick II, opened a new world when he introduced the computer and patiently walked me through many computer problems. My daughter, Elaine Irtz Metzger, and another son, Theodore (Ta–o) William, have supported and added to my collection. Additionally, my gracious neighbor and friend, Shelley Ferguson, has been a leaning post, always there for me to listen and advise.

Special recognition is given to nodder collectors whose enthusiasm and generosity have contributed so much encouragement in addition to many pictures from their own collections. There is no criteria to determine how many nodders are out there. This endeavor is a beginning.

I am grateful to a host of friends who have graciously welcomed me into their homes to view and also photograph their collections. I have received many letters from collectors throughout the United States and foreign countries, often including pictures, asking questions, seeking information, and a book!

Thus, multiple factors contributed to my research. Data has been compiled from libraries, museums, correspondence, other collectors, antique shops, dealers, and travels across the United States and foreign countries.

The eastern sector of Germany was a hub of manufactories, but World War II closed this to the outside world for forty years. Now reopened, hopefully more information will be forthcoming.

The Strong Museum in Rochester, New York, has the largest exhibit of nodders. I was privileged to view, research, and compare records from the collection of Margaret Woodbury Strong (1897 – 1969). She was a fascinating lady, born into a wealthy family and thus financially able to acquire many things that fascinated her from childhood. It was her early dream and life-long ambition that her treasurers would be housed in a museum for others to enjoy. Her nodder exhibit in the museum is outstanding.

The Lexington Public Library and the University of Kentucky Library have obtained books from outside sources. The New York Public Library researched additional requests for data.

This diversified coverage of nodding figurines ranges from fine objets d'art to mundane objets d'art, from the very expensive to the very inexpensive. The majority of nodders within this text are mine. Friends have graciously permitted inclusion from their collections.

Any discrepancies within these pages occur from available information, or the lack of thorough research. From limited resources I have drawn conclusions, and errors of judgement are mine. Opinions vary from whatever one chooses to believe. Whereas I have a lengthy bibliography, which I highly recommend, much study has been necessary to obtain this limited amount of data.

Values in this book are for use as a guide. They are based on a common denominator of availability, demand, condition, or rarity. Collectors recognize these variables. Values vary in different sections of the country. At auction, bidders set the price. But purchase from a private owner is strictly between buyer and seller. Other factors include house, estate, garage, and yard sales. Future values become more realistic as nodder enthusiasm warrants.

"Those in the know" do not always agree, and I am in the midst of them. Oscar Wilde said it so aptly, "The man who sees both sides of a question is a man who sees nothing at all."

This author disclaims responsibility for decisions the reader may reach. To my knowledge, this book is a first.

How was I to know a cheerful cook would take me on an endless journey? Thirty years ago she was grinning at me in an antique shop. The dealer called her a nodder. He touched her head, she said "Yes," and I brought her home. She was Victorian and had come from Germany. That was the extent of the dealer's information. She is 7" tall. (See Plate 1.)

Plate 1

Curiosity aroused, I consulted an old standby, my *Webster's New World Dictionary* from college days. I found "Nodder (nod´ ẽr), n. a person or thing that nods." But I already knew that. What I didn't know is that nodder is not in every dictionary. I looked. So I went to the library, that fount of information. I couldn't find a book on nodders. I checked indexed references, again, nothing.

It is no secret to my family that I am somewhat strong-minded — stubborn. In physics we learned that when an animate object meets an inanimate object, motion results from force of gravity. Thus, a gentle touch, a breeze, or vibration, like the nodder, produces motion.

Basically the nodder consists of two or more components manufactured from separate molds designed and balanced to go together and enhance movement. To the purist, a true nodder is set in motion by force of gravity. Thus it is neither wind-up, mechanical, electrical, nor frictional. A counterbalanced weight inside the body cavity is comparable to a bell clapper or the pendulum of a clock. A perfectly balanced nodder produced continuous motion for thirty minutes and longer, but this is rarely found among nodders today.

Unique methods to produce movement are discussed in this chapter. Collections may be eclectic or limited within a category. Very old nodders and the fine glazed porcelains are rare and rarely available. Many are in museums and private collections.

Nodders are of varied composition. They may be found in porcelain, bisque, ivory, pottery, ceramic, papier-mâché, composition, metal, wood, celluloid, plastic, or even pressed cardboard. During the mid-nineteenth century, Germany manufactured many for export. Others were used in games of chance or as giveaways at the circus and fairs. Finer specimens were marketed through shops and catalogs.

The "pin" through the cook's neck in Plate 2 is visible on her shoulder line. This sturdy piece of metal is also referred to as a "wire," or "shaft" and serves as a fulcrum to balance the cook's head from the extended pencil-shaped post that acts as the counterweight inside her body. (See Plate 3.) When the post is lowered through the aperture, the pin pivots on grooved shoulders, thus her head nods back and forth in a yes motion. During the Victorian era a flat piece of metal was generally used for this purpose. A round pin placed in the rectangular opening (on the neck) is indicative of a replaced wire.

Plate 2

Plate 4

Nodding figurines were modeled as modest folks to fine folks, as caricatures, Orientalia, children, and a variety of animals. Nodder pairs are desirable although frequently unattainable. Chinese craftsmen bequeathed a legacy valued yet today because much of their work was produced in pairs. True pairs go together but are not identical. When possible I purchase one good specimen in anticipation of later finding the missing mate.

The two 6¼" Staffordshire-type children with wire-rim glasses in Plate 4 are a true matching pair. The lad carries a walking stick, the girl an umbrella. Breakage and careless handling separated sets such as these, or merchants have been known to sell only one from the pair.

Conversely, the 3½" nodders in Plate 5 are look-alikes, but not a matching pair. Nodding action is produced from a pin through the neck. It rests on a pair of wires (visible beneath the collar) extending through the body from front to back.

Plate 3

Plate 5

This pin is not visible in the picture.

Nodder function was enhanced in various ways by the modeler's creativity and ingenious methods to produce motion.

Plate 6

Plate 7

Rather than a neck wire there is another common pivot. "Wings," molded on this post rest on the aperture and produce a nod. The ceramic salt and pepper shakers in Plates 6 and 7 are a pair of nodding trout, swimming in a squarish box decorated with flowers and scenes. One trout, removed, shows the part for condiment containment. Salt and pepper holes are on the back of the fish.

Condition and age are determinants, but irrespective of age, desirability is in the eye of the beholder. The McKinley Tariff Act provides clues as to age, but not always answers. The Act was so named because William McKinley, who was Ways and Means Chairman in the House of Representatives, sponsored the bill in Congress. Taxes on tobacco and alcohol were

reduced, but tariff duties on other products were raised appreciably, with protection the primary purpose.

Dated October 1, 1890, Chapter 1244, Section 6 states:

"That on or after the first day of March eighteen hundred ninety-one, all articles of foreign manufacture, such as are usually or ordinarily marked, stamped, branded or labeled, and all packages containing such or other imported articles, shall, respectively, be plainly marked, stamped, branded or labeled in legible English words so as to indicate the country of their origin; and unless so marked, stamped, branded, or labeled they shall not be admitted to entry."

A conclusion was issued to customs officers:

"In case of small articles which cannot be readily marked, the marking of inside cartons and outside packages will be sufficient."

Logically, nodders fall under the category of "small articles which cannot be readily marked." This accounts for many nodders lacking marks of identification and a false assumption that no mark predates an object prior to 1891.

If our antique nodders were produced in quantity, many did not survive as did their counterparts, i.e the statuesque "frozen" figurines (meaning no movable parts). Several reasons contribute to their scarcity.

Nodders are not as well known and consequently exist on today's endangered list. Unlike frozen figurines, nodders required considerable patience and skill to mold the separate parts to completion and final firing. Consequently, pieces emerged from the kiln in warped or damaged condition. Also, to produce motion and balance the counterweights required a precision and dexterity not germane to every modeler. Today's collector who attempts restoration of a damaged nodder learns that repositioning weights is no small feat. Conceivably, damaged parts became obsolete and in time were discarded.

OTHER EXAMPLES OF CONSTRUCTION

To the casual observer, nodders may appear the same, but interior construction is not. Therefore diverse methods to produce gravitational motion are exemplified here.

Plate 9

Plate 8

In Plate 8 the weighted 6" nodder is a magot, (māy go) or a female buddha. Her head is counterbalanced from a cylindrical weight of heavy lead alloy that is attached to a threaded brass rod, shown in Plate 9. Screwing this weight up or down controlled duration of movement. The threaded rod is anchored twice inside her neck. Note the visible flat pin protruding through the neck and a second visible mark below this pin to further secure the heavy cylinder weight. A mechanism inside the head is attached via a screw at the widow's peak and produces the in and

out movement of the tongue. Hands wave from a metal counterweight inside the sleeve. Thus she nods, wags her tongue, and waves her hands.

Another example shows two entirely different weights, exemplified by the 5¼" sage in Plate 10. The weight inside the sage's body, Plate 11, is a large glob of reddish-tone bisque that counterbalances the nodding head while the hand waves from a small pencil-post. For nodders with multiple moving parts, modelers devised a variety of weights to activate movement.

Plate 10

Plate 11

Plate 14

Plate 15

This serene 2½" Chinaman, in Plates 12 and 13, is sitting with his legs crossed. He is classified as a miniature (less than 3 inches). A tear-drop shaped counterweight supports a neck-pin that rests on a pair of cross wires through his collar from front to back and are thus invisible. He is a lively nodder. Also of interest, his clothes are painted, fired, and finished in bisque while his head, collar, hands, fan, and feet are glazed a lovely neutral ivory tone.

support a swaying motion. This idea of movement and balance was not novel. Centuries ago it was known and used in the Orient.

Plates 12 and 13

Plate 16

Plates 14 and 15 are caricatures of a comical 3" Chinaman. Body and head balance on pointed spikes. There is no pin. The head twirls on the body. The body rests on feet, sways and twirls around in dual motion.

These charming 3½" Dutch children, Plate 16, are also swayers with different construction. Their bodies rest on a similar pedestal. A wire pin at the waistline protrudes through the body and pedestal feet

This 11" reclining boxer in Plate 17 is a head-hanger. The boxer's head, Plate 18, nods, swings, and sways from an extended neck that is weighted and serves to counterbalance movement. An angled wire connects the head at the neck apex. This flocked papier-mâché dog has glass eyes,

Plate 17

Plate 18

Plate 20

natural markings, and a metal dog collar. During the mid-twentieth century these animated animals were popularly seen in automobile windows. Many came from Germany and are so marked. Copies from Japan, Hong Kong, and Taiwan are not infrequent and the quality ranges from excellent to poor.

This 3" miniature pair of Dutch children in Plate 19 are known as knotters

because the head is attached to the body by an elastic cord. Some collectors also refer to them as nodders and/or dolls.

Gran and Gup are a pair of bobbin' heads exemplified in Plate 20. They are highly glazed ceramic. A coil spring in the neck is completely concealed for lively movement. Also, their barely 2½" height classifies them as miniatures. Small pairs such as these are appearing on the market and collecting them today is timely.

The 4¼" metal jockey in Plate 21 illustrates another kind of construction. A concealed flexible steel strap connects his enlarged head and body cavity. The three-legged stool supports his weight and produces good nodding action.

Plate 19

Plate 21

Plate 22

lectible because many nodders were unmarked. Collectors may distinguish characteristic work of certain manufactories, but incised mold numbers, occasional initials, or artist brush marks were more of an aid to the manufactory and record of worker's output on payday. Records were not kept for posterity.

Married or mis-matched. (Mating two parts, not original.) We see this occasionally, as exemplified in Plate 22, and wouldn't you know, they are excellent nodders!

Plates 23 and 24 show another example. The back view reveals the head of a Japanese gentleman who would never wear that kimono wrapped with an obi.

Price. The caveats mentioned influence cost. But bottom line is agreement between buyer and seller. This varies in

CAVEATS

Who does not opt for mint quality? Because figurines with movable parts depart from this norm, many are no longer in fine condition. Unless you will consider a less than perfect specimen, you may never become a nodder collector.

Availability. Limited. Although the majority of early nodders were manufactured during the Victorian era, there is no record of mass production. The focal point was Germany but that is not to say nodders were not made elsewhere. By the turn of the century Japan got into the act. Search antique shops, shows, flea markets, and garage sales. And ask.

Condition vs Quality. Examine for chips, missing/replaced wires, and/or weights. If replaced, check for balance and movement. Damage may have been professionally restored, obvious, and/or acceptable at the discretion of the collector. Minimal or barely visible firing fractures are not uncommon. Finer quality retains original appearance and enhanced value, whereas value is diminished on work of lesser quality.

Marks. Few. Here is a unique col-

Plate 23

Plate 24

times with a fan), bodies sway, heads bounce, and feet wiggle. Whether construction and movement are simple or complicated, nodders radiate personality and become charming actors for family and friends.

Within the pages of this book, collectors will find a diversity of pleasing artifacts created by modelers and artists throughout several centuries. Research on the subject of nodders is ardently sought by the beginner to the advanced collector.

This is the purpose of my book.

different sections of the country. Estimated price guide values are just that, an estimate of cost, not necessarily its worth.

Repairs. Neither uncommon nor objectionable, if well done. After all, only so many were manufactured and continue to exist. With few exceptions, unlike some popular collectibles, early nodders have been copied but not reproduced. One exception, for example, the Meissen factory accepts a special order for the seated buddha that was originally manufactured in the 1700s. However, there is a two year waiting period, Meissen requires a substantial down payment, and the cost is in five figures.

Nodding figurines radiate dignified, whimsical, and comical personalities from expressive facial features, body language, and suggestive movable parts. Heads nod in a yes (front to back) or no (side to side) motion. Tongues wag, hands wave (some-

A STAIRSTEP OF NODDING BUDDAHS

Plate 25. Left to right: Pagod attributed to Carl Thieme, 9½"; Magot attributed to Meissen, 7¾"; Pagod attributed to Casper Wegley, 6"; Magot attributed to Meissen, 6"; Pagod attributed to Ernst Böhne, 4½". Prices not available.

EARLY BACKGROUND

Early porcelain of crude substance was known to the Chinese more than a thousand years ago, dating from the H'an dynasty (206 B.C. – 220 A.D.). By the Tang dynasty (618 – 907 A.D.) porcelain of finer quality had been perfected and remained a closely guarded secret for centuries. The Chinese equated the quality of porcelain with their jade. Artifacts and treasures were buried with reigning monarchs and important personages.

This exquisite pair of porcelain nodding Pagodas are mint. (See Plate 26.) They were a special order from the Meissen manufactory and recently arrived from Meissen, Germany, after a lengthy waiting period. The original molds from which they were manufactured date back to the eighteenth century. Original molds are still used, but the former Albrechtsburg factory site was transferred to its present location in the Triebischtal.

As background history of porcelain evolves in this chapter, the reader will gain insight to the evolution of these remarkable nodders.

Early nodders in the form of a seated Buddha, sometimes grotesque in appearance, are believed to have originated in Chinese temples during the late seventeenth century reign of K'ang Hsi, 1662 – 1722. A distinct feature was the movable

Plate 26. Barefoot Buddhas. Heads of the pair nod yes, tongues wag, and hands wave. Bare feet have turned-up toes. Their chinoiserie style is noted later in the chapter. Size is not identical, one is 8½" and the other is slightly smaller, 7¾". Mark of the underglaze blue Meissen crossed sword is inside the neck and at the base of each figurine. Circa August, 1995. Meissen, Germany. $5,000.00 each. Note: On pairs, feet will be crossed in reverse position.

Plate 27. Pu-tü, a happy Buddha of Chinese lore is joyful and fortunate because he has five sons. He is a frozen figurine, but would be a delightful nodder if he could nod harmoniously with his five frolicking boys. Tung Chih reign, circa 1930s. $75.00.

head and hands perfectly weighted and balanced to activate motion from the slightest vibration. A century later the replica of a grotesque nodding figurine with animated head, tongue, and hands was modeled at the Meissen factory, reflecting early influence of the East Asian style.

Pagodas are temples of multiple levels with a pyramidal peak. The Buddha, or Pagod, was a deity of the pagoda. The Magot, or poussah, refers to the female Buddha. Whether pagods were porcellanous, carved from wood, ivory, or jade, the nodding action was activated from perfectly balanced multiple parts.

Possibly the first porcelain to leave China was never intended for future mass production. Marco Polo sailed from Venice in 1271 for the Far East to search for spices and explore wonders of the ancient world. Among those wonders was porcelain. He was so captivated by the cultural and technological advances of the Chinese peoples his stay was prolonged many years. His diary recorded that nothing written was false because he personally witnessed this mysterious land of palaces and romantic gardens. He wrote fascinating tales of translucent porcelain dishes, bowls, and cups he called "Porcellana" (Portuguese for the glossy white cowrieshell). Twenty-five years later he returned to Venice with fantastic tales of another world, and an exquisite wonder, called china.

Vasco de Gama sailed from Portugal around the Cape of Good Hope in 1498. His ships landed at Canton where he established trade routes with southeastern Asia. A variety of exports included fabulous jewels, exotic spices, tea, lacquers, fabrics, wallpaper, furniture, citrus and plants, and especially porcelain. Storage of china, the weightier cargo, provided ballast in the ship's hull whereas lighter weight spices and tea were stored above to avoid moisture damage. China (dishes) was expendable. The crew reportedly used and tossed it into the sea. Pirating from other ships created additional hazard.

During the Middle Ages products trickled into Europe through returning missionaries and travelers. Missionaries went to save souls; crusaders sought trade and adventure. Trade flourished after the Dutch founded the East India Company in 1602, and by the end of the Ming dynasty markets from southern China and Japan had been established. Whereas porcelain was most desirable, it remained a technical mystery to European craftsmen. Quality was so superior it was simply referred to as "china."

Thus Europe was introduced to porcelain and the Europeans were impressed. To partake of exotic "three pleasant warm drinks," namely tea, cocoa, and chocolate, necessitated a functional container worthy of the libation — a china cup! Chinamania was not only a display of opulence but a show of culture. Those who could afford indulgence amassed quantities as symbols of wealth. Those who could not reflected with astonishment and admiration.

China was agreeable to export of her product but the secret remained a mystery. The Chinese Emperor believed the Celestial Empire had everything. He placed no value on strange objects, nor did he trust the outside world. He believed uncultured Europeans had no comparable trade.

Foreign exports from the Eastern world intrigued Augustus the Strong who was King of Poland, the Elector of Saxony, Friedreich Augustus II. European alchemists had struggled for several centuries to learn this secret and craftsmen were now inspired to intensify research.

A teamwork of three men, "a contubernium," were forerunners in a successful breakthrough of the porcelain secret. They were Johann Friedreich Böttger who was a chemist, Count Ehrenfried Walther von Tschirnhausen, a physicist, and the Freiberg Mine Councillor, Gottfreid Pabst von Ohain. The financial backer was the ambitious and artistically sensitive Augustus II.

Background history of these pioneers developed into extensive and interesting research for this book.

JOHANN FRIEDREICH BÖTTGER, 1682 – 1719

Born of Russian parentage in the town of Schleiz, Thuringia, Böttger's family moved to Magdeburg in search of opportunity for their talented son. His early fascination and aptitudes were in the field of chemistry, so by the age of 16 he was apprenticed to Friedreich Zorn, an apothecary in Berlin. Young Böttger's contacts and chicanery circulated rumors of his innate ability to transmute metal into gold and the intrigued King of Prussia requested an audience. Instead, Böttger fled Berlin for Dresden under escort of the King of Poland's cavalry. However, at Dresden the 19-year-old chemist became the king's prisoner, forced to work under difficult conditions.

As Böttger's efforts to produce gold were destined for failure, experiments with clay followed.

The first true hard paste was in 1708 – 1709, a red stoneware similar to the Chinese "Yi hsing." The next year Böttger informed Augustus that among his other inventions he had perfected a porcelain (a white hard-paste), the first in Europe which he declared was as good as the East Asian, if not superior. Also, it had "a hardness superior to that of marble." Above the portal of Böttger's workroom was an inscription (translated from German) "God, our Creator, has turned a goldmaker into a potter."

Tschirnhausen died in the interim. Other alchemists worked at the factory but credit is given to Böttger and it came to be known as "Böttgersteinzeug," Böttger porcelain. Extensive notes on experiments were in Böttger's handwriting. Work was conducted in the old Albrechtsburg castle (Albert's fortress, named after the Duke Albert the Brave, 1486 – 1500) overlooking the town of Meissen on the Elbe River, 14 miles east of Dresden. Every room was painted with a threat, "Be secret unto death."

Equally significant and timely was the use of alabaster and a local clay mineral deposit akin to kaolin. The mass fused while baking and became impermeable. The secret housed in the Albrechtsburg manufactory was to have been zealously guarded by a privileged few (they were called arcanists, guardians of the secret formula). But nomadic artists and workmen defected, were fired, or hired away by rivals, taking their knowledge with them.

The talented Böttger was unpopular with co-workers, and from his irregular life-style he died an alcoholic nine years after the manufactory was founded.

Johann Gregor Höroldt, who had worked in a Vienna factory was hired as artist director at Dresden and proved to be one of the great masters of his day. His ability and leadership was a dominant factor in the success of the Meissen factory.

Early European potters copied Chinese wares in the chinoiserie style including figurines with a moving head, open mouth, tongue, and waving hands. Although much of their early work emerged from the kiln in damaged condition, Meissen influence and porcelain was the envy of all other European manufactories.

Production of the chinoiserie nodding magot (the female Buddha, pronounced may´–go) and pagod (the male Buddha, pronounced pay´–go) in the Buddhist style continues at the Meissen factory to the present day. Comparison of Plate 26 with the earlier Meissen nodders, in Plate 28, is remarkable. They are excellent figurines with nodding heads, wagging tongues, large pendulous ears, and waving hands. They remain unchanged and are produced from original molds in several sizes. Special orders for the pagoda require a lengthy waiting period and a five-figure price tag.

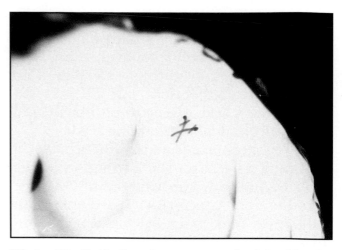

Plate 29. Both figurines are marked inside the body and neck with the underglaze blue Elector's sword, the oldest and best known mark of quality and still in use today. By 1724 the trademark was adopted into general use as coat-of-arms for the Saxon rulers. Similar marks were counterfeited by other factories until the end of the nineteenth century when Meissen was granted the national and international copyright trademark.

Plate 28. Two Meissen magots in chinoiserie style, identical in size, but different polychrome decoration. 6". Marked with blue underglaze crossed swords. Hard-paste porcelain. They are attributed to Johann Friedreich Eberlein, a sculptor and modeler at Meissen from 1739 to 1749. There is no artist signature as this was not customary. However, some artist's work may be recognized by distinction of the piece. Excellent condition. $5,000.00 – 6,000.00 each.

Plate 30. The magots have Chinese characteristics. A cylindrical lead weight is suspended inside the rotund body. The figurines sit with feet crossed at the ankles. Slanted eyes and brows, oversize pendulous ears, and a gleeful grin expose a full set of teeth. Hands wave with well formed fingers and fingernails. Touch the head for a nod and the tongue wags. A widow's peak outlines the forehead. Dark hair, streaked with gray, is pulled in a twist at the crown in contrast to the pagod's smooth hair style.

Plate 31. The 6" nodding porcelain pagod has a smooth hair style. His head nods with animated tongue and waving hands. Large ears stand out from his head but are not pendulous. The zinc weight with screw adjustment regulates movement. $500.00.

Plate 33. A large pair of chinoiserie pagods, by Carl Thieme, 9½". Saxon Porcelain Factory. Germany. Circa late 1800s to present. Hard-paste porcelain. These large Buddhas are recognized with pendulous ears, happy facial features, and typical body contour. A gentle touch produces a nod of the head and the metal tongue wags with a clanking sound. Hands with detailed fingers and nails wave up and down. The magot has gray hair, a widow's peak, topknot at the crown of her head, wide grin, and full set of teeth. Her garment has slipped from the left shoulder and she sits with her left foot over the right one. Polychrome colors of this pair are clear and bright.

The pagod has like facial features and smooth dark hair. His robe has slipped from both shoulders and separated in front to expose his fat belly. His feet are reversed from hers. Cavernous bodies of these nodders provide ample space for liberal counter-movement of the weighted head. Nodding action from heavy cylindrical metal counterweights emits a dull tone and classifies this pair among bell collectors as nodder-bells.

This exceptional pair of matching Buddhas are in pristine condition. Close examination reveals Thieme's work to be of good quality, but not comparable to that of Meissen. $2,500.00 – 3,500.00 pair.

Plate 32. A mark inside the body appears to be Wilhelm Casper Wegley, 1751 – 1757. Prussian King Frederick the Great granted Wegley a work permit, but the privilege was revoked and Wegley was forced to close, dating this excellent nodder in the mid-eighteenth century.

Plates 34 and 35. The blue underglaze mark belongs to Carl Thieme, a Dresden manufacturer. His mark, is located at the back and near the base of each figurine.

Plate 37. Mark of Carl Thieme.

Plate 36. This young Chinese lad could become a budding Buddha with his happy stride and round belly, 8½". Wearing a green-leaf hat on his nodding head, he is dressed in the chinoiserie style. Mold No. 8812. Unusual and excellent condition. $400.00 – 500.00.

CARL THIEME

A word here about Carl Thieme, his factory, and operations. In 1867 he opened a shop in Potschappel about 25 miles from Dresden. His original porcelain blanks were purchased from other factories and often decorated in the Meissen manner with an applied mark that closely resembled Meissen. With or without intent, Thieme surely held Meissen in high regard because his efforts imitated the product as well as the mark. Before copyright was granted for the Electoral sword, similarity of Thieme's work and marks, and that of other artists, were in constant conflict with Meissen.

Meissen considered Thieme a charlatan, a forger, and thorn in their side. Thieme began his own porcelain production in 1872, and work was subsequently carried on by his family. Quality has variously been described as good to excellent, but his ruthless tactics were deceptive, specifically the similarity of his factory marks with those of Meissen. Dresden identification was a magic connotation that enhanced sales for the English and American markets. In England it was referred to as Dresden, while in France it was Porcelains De Saxe. Thieme's mark was eventually approved in 1901. The mark, printed with or without a crown, is among several used by the Thieme factory.

 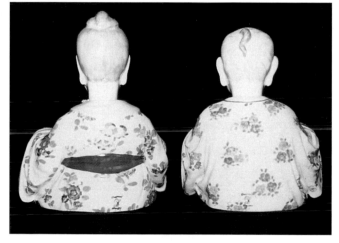

Plates 38 and 39. Chinese porcelain pair in chinoiserie style, 7¼". Underglaze blue Dresden mark of Carl Thieme. Circa late 1800s to present. No price available.

This beautiful pair nod yes and wave hands. They have a happy smile, dimpled cheeks, and fine set of teeth. Their fair countenance contrasts slanted eyes and brows, oversize ears, and a Fu Manchu mustache. His hair is carefully groomed in a queue, while hers is pulled in a topknot at the crown of her head. Their legs are crossed at the ankle in reverse position and slippers have pointed turned-up toes. Their elaborate chinoiserie robes drape gracefully over silk pantaloons. Lead counterweights produce a dull clapper sound when activated, like nodder-bells. Around 1800 potters added a mixture of bone ash with other ingredients. This bone-ash mixture versus the earlier kaolin-feldspar mixture produced a different bell tone.

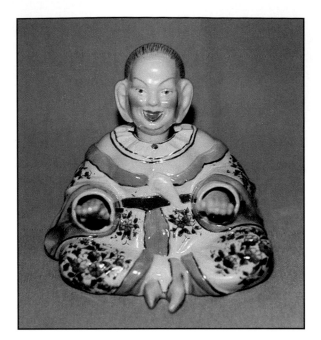

Plate 40. A charming small porcelain Buddha, 4½" and copy of Meissen work. Head and hand movement is produced from lead counterweights. The pagod's smooth hairline is receding and a frozen tongue is visible between parted lips. This pristine nodder is completely original to a fine flat neck pin and arm wires. Mark of Ernst Bohne Sons. $550.00+.

Plates 42 and 43. Front and side views of a bronze nodding Buddha. 5¼". It weighs 3⅝ lbs, which is heavy for a nodder of this size. The mark embossed on the base: Tiffany Studios, Broadway New York. Circa 1970s. $950.00.

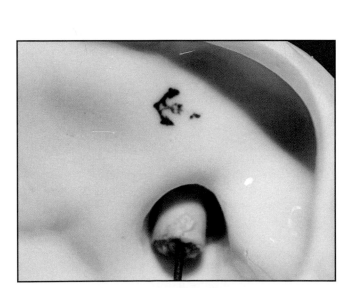

Plate 41. The dark blue underglaze mark of Ernst Bohne Sons, Rudolstadt. Circa 1878 – 1920.

I began research on this bronze nodding Buddha from the day I bid at auction. Tiffany Studios was a mysterious mark. An interesting saga was to follow. According to the auctioneer, the deceased owner purchased this Buddha in an antique shop in New York City. Possibly true. A legible paper sticker on the base reads, "a rare find." Untrue. The dictionary defines rare as uncommon and unusual which puzzling circumstances substantiate.

The Tiffany name denotes fine art. The detailed casting and quality are excellent. Components were assembled with precision. Four screws fasten a base plate that can be removed to reveal evidence of residual wax from the casting. Strong weights and wires connect inside the body to activate movement. Pushing the head back starts simultaneous movement of the head, long pointed tongue, and hands.

Although nodding action is somewhat brief, hands raise together in a "Praise Allah" gesture. Three screws anchor the neck collar almost concealing a wire that pierces the neck. Weight for the wagging tongue is concealed inside the head. Ear lobes are pendulous. Eyes and brows are slanted. Prominent upper and lower teeth are molded on the overshot pointed jaw. Pointed-toe shoes repeat the same floral design embossed on the garment.

Buddha is comprised of a number of molded bronze parts: head, tongue, body, collar, base plate, a pair of hands, plus screws, sturdy wires, and weights. Compared to the nodder-bell, a dull tone sounds as the weight strikes inside the bulbous body.

I am indebted to research from the New York Public Library. They sent conclusive evidence that this is not a product

Plate 44. A smaller bronze Buddha closely resembles Plate 42. This nodder was permanently anchored to the base. Marks, if any, were not visible. No clue as to the reason for the hole by the right hand. Price not available.

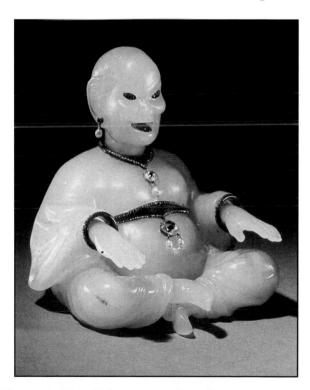

Plate 45. This Fabergé jewel, 3½", is an enameled bowenite figure of a nodding pagoda. Circa 1903 – 1914. An exquisite nodder, it was sold at auction in Geneva, Switzerland, on May 10, 1989, by Habsburg, Feldman, Ltd. Fine Art Auctioneers. The gavel fell on a final bid of $310,000.00.

of Tiffany Studio because records do not verify a Tiffany Studio on Broadway. *Trow's New York City Directory* records 1902 – 1903 at 333 4th Avenue as the first Tiffany Studio. This location was moved a number of times, and the last *Trow's Directory* of record in 1925 places Tiffany at 391 Madison Avenue. During the interim, a studio was never listed on Broadway.

This was obviously a pseudo mark. Research continued. Lewis Comfort Tiffany worked with metals as early as 1890, but his work with bronze was more after the turn of the century. Tiffany was a talented, demanding craftsman. His name denotes quality. He traveled extensively and collected Oriental items from the Far East. This bronze nodding Buddha favors earlier Meissen type work, and although it resembles Tiffany and bears the name, it is not a Tiffany product. Rather, around mid-1900 numerous artifacts of very good quality were manufactured in England and marketed in the States through auction houses and shops with implication of

authenticity. Many of these were marked "Tiffany, Broadway, New York." Some were unmarked. Others were marked "221 Regent St., London, England." Names of E. Gaylord and A.J. Nash were sometimes added. Therein was a clue. At one time Nash had been a registered artist at the Tiffany Studio. Fine workmanship is indisputable, and nodders reportedly were priced in four figures, but they are not antique. Adding to this intriguing bronze nodder...is it male or female, a magot or pagod? Receding hairline is masculine, but the nodding head rests on a bulbous body with pendulous breasts. Consider the alternate theory that equates pendulous breasts with the pagod's portly body.

Conclusion: This fine work of art is impressed with a pseudo mark, but interesting and quite desirable to the collector. Whenever you find Tiffany Studios, be alert. Items occasionally appear in shops and auctions with this mark. Extensive research exposes a scheme that turned a quick profit.

PETER CARL FABERGÉ, 1846 – 1920

Peter's father, Gustav, served apprenticeship to a jeweler before he opened his own shop on Morskaya Street in St. Petersburg. Later he left the shop in charge of a manager and moved his family to Dresden. In Dresden Peter Carl and younger brother, Agathon, whiled away pleasant hours at the Green Vault (Grüens Gewölbe), a museum that displayed articulated toys.

Fabergé was educated in Europe and apprenticed into the goldsmith's craft to follow the footsteps of his talented father. On extensive travels he observed work of great artists. When he settled in St. Petersburg he was well qualified to assume control of his father's business. Many skilled craftsmen worked under his close observation and the business expanded to other cities.

Perhaps Fabergé is best known for a sequence of magnificent Imperial Easter eggs produced for the ill-fated Romanov court. His renown in the latter half of the nineteenth century as a foremost goldsmith and jeweler is well documented. However it is Fabergé's nodding pagoda that intrigues the nodder collector. Perhaps visits to the Green Vault made a lasting impression in the form of four nodding pagodas in existence today.

The cheerful Buddha in Plate 45 surely intrigued Peter Carl Faberge because later in his career he produced four jeweled nodders of fine gemstone quality. The fact that these fabulous treasures are well documented is unusual and rare.

The Habsburg, Feldman's auction catalog (1989) listed "a Fabergé highly important jeweled and enameled bowenite figure of a pagoda." The nodder is unmarked. However, it came with the original fitted case, stamped "Fabergé, St. Petersburg, Moscow, London."

These three cities date this pagoda between 1903 and 1914. Records indicate that although the original location of the St. Petersburg shop moved and expanded, it was in business until forced closure in 1918 as a result of the Bolshevik Revolution. A Moscow branch had opened in 1887. The London branch opened in 1903 but closed with the outbreak of World War I. That places Plate 45 within a 1903 – 1914 time frame. During this period the name of Henrick Wigstrom surfaced as head workmaster in the St. Petersburg shop. Wigstrom had taken charge in 1903 after the death of his predecessor, Michael Evlampievich Perchin.

Name of the new owner of this pagoda is unavailable, but the interesting description of Plate 45 in the auction catalog is as follows:

"The seated Chinaman, with mobile head, hands, and cabochon ruby tongue, with ruby eyes, red guilloche enamel waistband, collar and cuffs, with two large faceted diamonds, suspended at neck and waist each with pearls beneath ruby and pearl ear pendants."

The three remaining pagodas briefly described in the catalog are in private collections.

(1) Her Majesty, the Queen Elizabeth. 6⅝". Rose quartz body with dark chalcedony head and hands.
(2) Lady DeGrey. 5¼". Bowenite, similar to Plate 45.
(3) Private collection in the United States. 5⅝". Pale green jadeite.

NODDER BELLS

Nodding pagodas intrigue bell collectors. Ample expanse inside the porcelain body permits the clapper-weight to strike a simulated bell tone, not so much like a bell, but rather a clacking sound. The nodder's counterweight relates to the bell clapper. Fine porcelain bells ring with a beautiful melodic tone and are collected in many forms other than the traditional bell that readily comes to mind. The pagod is an example.

Members of American Bell Association International, Inc. II (ABAII) collect a variety of bells. Their annual conventions are well attended and various regional chapters hold area meetings throughout the year. *The Bell Tower* is their bi-monthly publication.

Plate 46. A brass nodder bell, 4¾". This Victorian lady's bonnet frames her beautiful face. Her bouffant skirt is softly pleated and cloaked with a wrap-around shawl. Neck pin is not original. $150.00.

Plate 47. Three of five nodder-bells cast by the "Lost Wax" method — Friar Tuck, La Esmeralda, and Santa Claus. They were designed, sculpted, and handmade of highest quality bronze by Gerry Ballantyne of Overland Park, Kansas. They are in mint condition, serially numbered, signed, and registered Ballantyne Specialties ©.

Friar Tuck was the legendary monk immortalized in the adventures of Robin Hood. Exploits of Robin Hood's gang tamed the laws of Sherwood forest. Mythical, fanciful, and historical tales are repeated in ballad, poetry, and literature. Friar Tuck is No. 27 from a limited edition of 500. Circa 1979. © Gerry Ballantyne. $275.00.

La Esmeralda is a charming double nodder-bell. As she dances, her head nods and a dainty toe taps the edge of her skirt, producing the bell ring which Ballantyne says is not really the nicest bell tone because she dances on a solid base. But dance she truly does, and continues her act a minimum of one thousand times. La Esmeralda's tragic life began as an infant. Stolen by a Gypsy tribe, she lived in the worst slums of Paris. Her beauty and lively song and dance attracted large crowds and especially the ardor of Frollo, arch deacon of Notre Dame. Quasimodo, the bell ringer of Notre Dame, also loved and befriended her and once saved her life, but he was so ugly and deformed she could not bear his sight. Nor could she accept advances from the evil priest Frollo. Eventually Esmeralda was falsely accused of witchcraft and executed. In *Hunchback of Notre Dame*, she was Victor Hugo's heroine. Esmeralda is No. 329 from a limited edition of 400. Circa 1983. © Gerry Ballantyne. $300.00.

The style of Santa's long-belted coat dates prior to the turn of the century. With a bag of toys for good little girls and boys he announced his arrival by ringing the bell and nodding his head. 5" and 1 lb 9oz. He is No. 197 from a limited edition of 300 bells. Circa 1989. © Gerry Ballantyne. $250.00.

Plate 48. Three bronze nodder bells. They have great detail and comparatively heavy weight, but not the greatest nodders. The threaded connecting rod from the clapper screws inside the head.

Mama cat, sitting on an ornate cushion, is playing with her three kittens, 3½". The clapper is a round disk, 1⅓", and connects the head with a bronze wire. A pin through the neck rests on the aperture. Eighteenth century French bell. $500.00.

The young lad, 4½", sitting on a fancy cushion has raised his arm, wailing for attention because one broken leg of his puppet doll is laying between his legs. The clapper disk is 1". English, eighteenth century. $1,025.00.

The interesting little old landlady is walking the street hawking a room for rent. She is dressed in a long skirt, floral blouse, an apron with pockets, neck scarf, and mobcap. She holds keys in one hand and a sign in the other, "Chambr a loue," or room to rent, 4⅝". Her clapper disk measures ¾". French, eighteenth century. $500.00.

PORCELAIN OF LATE NINETEENTH AND EARLY TWENTIETH CENTURY

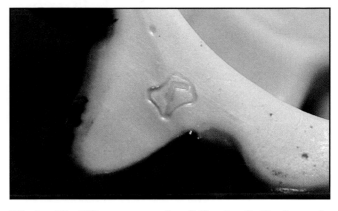

Plates 49 and 50. Chinese mandarin and his lady, modeled in fine glazed porcelain of translucent quality. 6". The elegant pair are dressed in silk. Molded detail is excellent with inside glazing. Matching pairs with identical mold numbers are not always found together.

Head and hands are well balanced with bisque counterweights. An anchored wire centered on the lady's headband, and the mandarin's hat brim, control tongue movement. His elaborate robe is befitting his position of authority in the Chinese government. The lady's intricate hair style is entwined in an elegant tiara. Her colorful robe is resplendent with Watteau drape down her back, pleated pantaloons, and high-button pointed-toe shoes. Oriental features are slanted eyes and brows and the mandrin's Fu Manchu mustache. Observe their legs are crossed in reverse. Condition is excellent except for one counterweight replacement of the lady's right hand. Mold number 5380 (on both). Conta and Boehme. Possneck (Thuringia, Germany). 1878 – 1930. $950.00+ per pair.

Plate 51. Elbogen mark of Conta & Boehme is impressed into the paste, no color.

Plate 52. Another exceptional pair painted and fired in bisque. Same size, mold, and maker, but different colors from the artist's pallet. Predominately aqua with delicate tint. $750.00 – 950.00.

Plate 53. A jolly anthropomorphic, 5". He's a highly glazed ceramic pig. He's a fat Buddha. He's dressed like Buddah. His head rocks on wings and says no. Unmarked. Possibly a product of China. $35.00 – 45.00.

GERMANY, EIGHTEENTH CENTURY
AREA OF PORCELAIN MANUFACTORIES

1. Magdeburg, the town where Böettger grew up.
2. Berlin, Böettger at the age of sixteen was apprenticed to Fredierich Zorn, an apothecary.
3. Dresden, nineteen year old Böettger left Berlin under protection of the King of Poland's cavalry.
4. Old Albrechtsburg Castle, site of porcelain factory.
5. Meissen, site of castle on Elbe River.
6. Colditz, source of mineral deposit in breakthrough of porcelain manufacture.
7. Possneck, area of Conta & Boehme factory.
8. Rudolstadt, area of Conta & Boehme factory.

Nodders in this chapter are of porcelain and "biscuit," or bisque, a vitrified unglazed porcelain fired once to a temperature reaching 1450°C (2650°F). Additional glazing and firing of porcelain make it shiny.

MEISSEN INFLUENCE

During the eighteenth century royalty and privileged wealthy aristocrats sponsored porcelain factories on the Continent. Artists and decorators acquired a marketable talent for pleasing Europeans, and the Meissen factory was at the forefront. Imitation of the chinoiserie style indicated European high regard for Chinese cultural arts and reflected taste and fashion of the day. Asian features of figurines with slanted eyes and brows were the early European concept — the Roman nose, narrow face, pointed chin, and Fu Manchu mustache.

The city of Meissen was an influential leader while the city of Dresden on the other side of the Elbe River was the cultural art center. Arcanists at the Meissen manufactory were not loyal, they defected and carried their knowledge of the secret with them. Furthermore, various forms of the Meissen electoral sword were profusely copied.

What about nodders?

References detail information about figurines, but recognition of the nodder per se is negligible. Many nodders "in the biscuit" were painted with enamel colors and fired a second time. Colors have diminished on works of lesser quality and firing cracks are not unusual. However, excellent workmanship of better manufactories is quality yet today. Gold accent increased intrinsic value and many early artists supplied their own gold. Nodders with a solid base may be of earlier vintage, but this is no criteria because nodders are found with an exposed body cavity and evidence of age as well.

Early Meissen and Dresden nodders are privately owned or in museums and rarely surface for sale. Nodders of later vintage are available from time to time, but subject matter and research are lacking.

Meissen's quality and beauty set a pattern of standards that exist to this present day. Because glazed porcelain and hard-paste were popular and successful, the European manufacturer did not make a transition to biscuit until the late eighteenth century.

Research is difficult because laws in that day did not require an imprint or mark, discussed in Construction of Nodders. Thus figurines are identified from study, comparison, and recognition. However, any visible evidence or mark on nodders are so noted in this text.

Plate 54. Oriental Chinoiserie lady (front view).

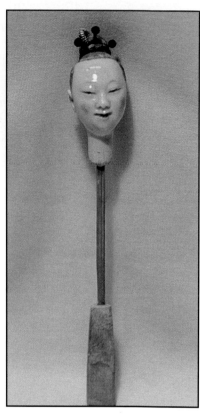

Plate 55, Plate 56, and Plate 57. Chinoiserie lady of noble birth resembling Chinese porcelain from the Ching Dynasty 1736 – 1795. She is German porcelain from the late seventeenth century and an exceptional nodding figurine. 23", weight 3 lbs. 7 oz. One of a kind.

This figurine is molded on a square socle surrounded on the four sides with coral-red flowers interspersed with green foliage within a coral-red border. Fragile hands and long slim fingers support the eight-sided vase decorated with acanthus leaves encircling the top and base.

Her delicate long face, high forehead, and exaggerated slanting eyelids narrowly open to reveal intense dark eyes. A faint smile appears on her red lips. Of significance, there is no neck pin, rather her slender neck rests on the collar of her robe while she nods with gentle dignity.

Her cobalt robe, embellished with gilt-outlined medallions, covers a coral-red dress with flowing sleeves. Turquoise cuffs complement the tied sash. Her yellow pleated skirt is trimmed with a cobalt border edged in gilt.

Long hair is intricately entwined at the crown of her head, affixed with three ornate pins.

MULTIPLE NODDERS, PAIRS, and SINGLES

Single nodders are the most common. Occasionally pairs nod together. Triples comprise one, two, and/or three nodding parts. Five nodding heads on a single mold are rare. Rarest of all is the figurine with multiple (six or more) nodding heads.

Plate 58. Chinese family of five, 5½". This handsome Chinese family is unusual and rare, comprising one solid mold with five heads nodding yes. Condition is excellent except for replacement of several wires. Colorful garments and detailed features make this an outstanding group. Fortunate parents, "lucky because they have three sons," stand with first-born between them while two younger sons sit at their feet. Each hold something: mother a scroll, father (with Fu Manchu mustache) a string instrument, eldest son a jar, and the younger boys a fan and pipe. Mother's dark hair is fashioned in a circular knot at the crown of her head and pierced with a gold ornament. The men wear conical bamboo hats. Slanting eyes and brows are Oriental, but the nose is Roman and the chin pointed. Semi-translucent bisque porcelain. $1,500.00 – 3,000.00.

Plate 59. Blue anchor mark of Ernst Bohne Söhne, showing the manufacturer's mark on the base of the Chinese family. Picture does not show entire base with counterweights. Rudolstadt, Thüringia, 1854 – 1920.

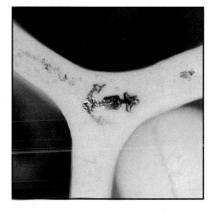

Plate 60. Tableau of seated Chinese family members. 3" – 4¾", (not including umbrellas). Same pear-shaped weights as Plate 63. Translucent bisque. Pair with umbrella, $200.00+. Others, $75.00 – 125.00 each.
  This tableau is an interesting comparison to Plate 58. The parents were acquired at the English flea markets and are unusual. The beautiful translucent umbrellas elevate their elite status. Reuniting the family over a period of several years was coincidental. The individual components were a surprise birthday gift from my late husband. The two sons holding fans were located, one on the East Coast and the other in the midwest. Tradition mandates that grandfather, the elder, is esteemed as older and wiser. He is holding an opium pipe and was the final gift to complete this family circle and the ultimate goal of any collector. Each nodder is in excellent condition. Features are finely detailed and pastel garments are color coordinated. Construction and nodding action are identical, including pear-shaped counterweights. Ernst Bohne Söhne, unmarked.

Plate 61. "Older and wiser," the same elders with opium pipes, one is miniature, 2¼", and the other one 3". Ernst Bohne Söhne, unmarked. Small, $125.00. Large, $200.00.

Plate 63. The base shows the five pear-shaped bisque counterweights and blue anchor mark of Ernst Bohne Söhne. Circa 1854 – 1920. Marks on the nodding Chinese family and the nodding Czarists are identical.

Plate 62. Another excellent and rare nodding group is a five-figure translucent bisque mold that has been equated to the tragic demise of the Romanov dynasty. 5¼" x 5¼". Nodding action and the mark are identical to the Ernst Bohne Söhne five-figure mold on the base of Plate 59. $1,500.00 – 3,000.00.

The Russian family appears warmly dressed in ankle length coats of sable-trimmed natural Manchurian ermine. Two children wear boots and sit with their pet dog. Nicholas is holding a long-handled butterfly net. Romanovs were related to the Russian Court by blood and intermarriage, thus the net the Czar holds gives meaning to his interest in entomology. They were an artistic and privileged family of nature lovers, credited for their hunt, research, identification, and cataloging butterfly and moth species in different parts of the world.

THE ROMONAVS

Herein is a legend concerning this controversial mold.

Five nodding heads relate to a historical event that occurred during the Bolshevik Revolution and has been researched to the present day. Did the modeler of this figurine at Bohne's factory have the Romonov's in mind — Czar Nicholas II, his unpopular German born wife, Czarina Alexandra, and their children? If this was the intent, three of their five children are in the mold. Four siblings were girls. Alexei, their only son and royal heir was a hemophiliac. At that time Gregory Rasputin, the Siberian peasant monk, was privy to the Romanov court and reportedly capable of curing Alexei's bleeding.

The fatal night for the Imperial family was July 16, 1918. All seven family members were executed in the basement of a house in Yekaterinburg where they had been held prisoner. Announcement in Moscow was not made public until two days later, on July 18. Ironically, within six weeks, on August 30th, an assignation attempt was made on Lenin's life. From that day, Lenin suffered severe health problems resulting in a series of strokes that led to his death in 1924. As the renowned Father of Communism, Lenin's tomb was in public view on the Red Square in Moscow with an hourly exchange of goose-stepping honor guards. President Boris Yeltsin eventually ordered removal of the guard on October 8, 1993, and the following month Lenin's embalmed body was interred elsewhere.

But, back to the ill-fated Romanov family. Their bodies were dumped in an abandoned salt mine of the Ural Mountains near Yekaterinburg. Reports (or rumors) circulated that Alexei, Maria, and youngest daughter Anastasia may have been injured, befriended, and escaped. Alexei, being a bleeder, would have required medical attention. In time, some rumors were silenced.

Legend and mystery concerning the youngest daughter, Grand Duchess Anastasia, persisted. Various women outside Russia claimed her identity. This fascinating odyssey inspired a Broadway play, a ballet, a musical, a TV drama, a biography, and numerous articles in the press. Interesting to note, the Ernst Bohne factory discontinued production two years after the Romanovs were executed.

A woman by the name Anastasia proclaimed to be the grand duchess until her demise in July 1984. Since then, DNA tests declared her claim void.

As recently as 1991 remains believed to be of the Czarist family were unearthed near Yekaterinburg and removed to Britain for further study. The scientific technique of DNA analysis through blood samples of blood-related Romanov kin conclude that the remains are of the Romanov family.

For centuries fans were used in the Orient. Late in the Han Dynasty a Chinese ruler, Hung Ming, achieved fame waving a large feather fan when presenting his new political stratagems. In addition to practicality, fans evolved into a fashionable accessory for ladies and gentlemen and their popularity is relevant to our nodders. Fans were ivory and lace, silk, feathers, parchment, and wood. With our nodders, fans were molded to the body, spread behind the head, or placed in one hand and set in motion by that gentle touch.

Coralene beading was another decorative Victorian touch used to enhance elegance. These tiny beads ranged from colorless to tinted, silver, or gilt and were fired with the figurine. Beading that was affixed with glue easily flaked off.

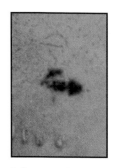

Plates 64, 65, and 66. Two views of a beautiful porcelain lady in excellent condition. An elaborate hairdo outlines the contour of her delicate oval face with slanted eyes and brows. Her elegant robe is bordered with fine embroidery. She is rare. The mark at the base is the blue anchor of Ernst Bohne Söhne (the same mark on the Chinese and Russian families). Thuringia, Germany, 1854 – 1920. No price available.

Plate 67 and 68. This buxom lady is Caucasian with an Oriental look, 3¾". She wears fine silk garments, jewelry, and much coralene beading. Her outstretched hands do not wave, but she nods an agreeable yes. No marks, probably Bohne. Bisque, late nineteenth century. $145.00.

Plate 69. A noble gentleman and his lady nod no. They sit cross-legged on the floor with open fans behind them. 6¼". Their lavish silk garments are well coordinated and they are excellent nodders. No marks. Germany. $600.00 – 795.00.

Plate 70. This beautiful bisque lady was admired by earlier gentry in the Bluegrass area, 6¾". Ownership of the nodder passed through several generations. During those years she was affectionately named and referred to as the well-known Madam Belle Brezing (1860 – 1940) of Lexington, Kentucky. (Source of information confidential.) She nods no. $300.00.

Plate 71. Young lad dressed in Japanese style, with a blond queue curled atop his head, 4¾". Fine translucent bisque porcelain in near mint condition. Impressed mold number 1589 – 90 and A.C. on the porcelain counterweight attached via a stick in the neck. Excellent detail and lovely pastel colors splattered with gold coralene beading. Left hand holds a fan. Unusual. Yes nodder via flat pin through the neck. $160.00 – 195.00.

Plates 72 and 73. Components of an aristocratic Japanese couple, assembled and dissembled as photographed, 8½". $950.00 as is.

A dealer acquired these separated parts through an estate sale, sans counterweights. He related a disastrous tale. He said the late owner was a bell collector who displayed the handsome pair with her bells, but did not enjoy their movement. Thus, the lady removed and apparently destroyed counterweights of this otherwise excellent pair. The dealer had no further information.

Each nodder was intended to wave one hand and open fan. Heads should nod yes. White skin tones contrast their Oriental features. The lady has a beautiful dimpled chin and her blonde curls are fashioned with an intricate hair ornament. The gentleman's blond queue is twisted at the crown with another ornament. Silk pantaloons are embossed with gold peacocks, butterflies, and a rooster. Lavish use of gold coralene beading typifies wealth. Even their shoes are fastened with gold buttons. After 1850. Germany.

Marks:

Plate 74. Excellent Meissen-type nodders, bisque porcelain with delicate trim, 6¼". Heads nod yes. Fans and hands wave. After 1850. $550.00+ per pair. Marks:

Plate 75. Family trio in a single mold, 3¾" x 7¼". Bisque porcelain. Mother on the right waves a fan that conceals her smirking countenance as she gossips with little daughter. Father in the center is nodding no–no. Germany. After 1850. $350.00 – 450.00.

Plate 76. Another family trio. Mother in the center holds an open fan behind her head and nods no. Father on the left is pointing his finger and waving a fan. Figure on the right in a coolie hat, nods yes but there is no fan in his right hand. Broken off, missing? $350.00 – 450.00+.

Plate 77. This same mold is painted as black Orientals. $475.00 – 525.00.

Plate 78. Another family trio is in pastel green tint. Size and nod of Plates 77 and 78 are the same mold as Plate 76, but both figures hold a fan in the right hand. $350.00 – 450.00+.

Plate 79. Miniature Chinese couples, translucent bisque porcelain. 1⅝". $75.00 each pair.

These delicate nodding pairs were manufactured in the area of Saxony around the turn of the century and discovered in a German warehouse in 1989. Thus their condition is pristine. They are painted in three color tones, ivory, mint, and Pompadour pink and closely resemble their larger counterparts. A flat neck pin resting on the aperture anchors round bisque counterweights attached in the neck via a wooden stick, typical construction of the Victorian era.

Plate 80. Another miniature pair molded in translucent porcelain, 2½". Light glazing but lavish gold decoration on collar and cuffs. Lady holds an open fan. He holds an opium pipe in his hand. Counterweight missing on the gentleman. $150.00 as is.

Plates 81. Translucent glazed porcelain couple nodding yes. The lady, 6½", has a match-striker basket on her back. The water carrier, 6¼", supports his weight as is the custom, with a yoke over his shoulders. Bisque pencil-shaped counterweights inside the body are attached via a wooden stick, with impressed mold numbers 7646, 7614K. The smaller Chinaman is carrying his containers on a yoke supported across one shoulder. 4¼". Germany, pre-1900. Small, $150.00. Large, $160.00 – 200.00 each.

Plate 82. Tableau of nodding figurals in the Art Nouveau style, 4½". Translucent bisque, delicately tinted and studded with gold coralene beading. Near mint condition. Mold numbers are impressed on porcelain pencil-shaped counterweights. The lad's large feather fan holds toothpicks. $400.00 – 500.00 per pair.

Plate 83. Elegant couple with large feather fans are dressed in green with gilt trim, 6¼". Bisque porcelain in excellent condition. Mold No 7662. $400.00 – 500.00 pair.

Plate 86. A matching couple clutching salt cellars in their arms. Salt cellars predate salt and pepper shakers and were in use as early as the sixteenth century. Nod yes, but maker unknown. Dealer believed them to be French, but are probably of German origin. Circa late 1800s. $300.00 – 450.00 pair.

Plates 84 and 85. The lady, with an open fan in her hand holds a match basket with striker sides. 6½". Glazed porcelain in cobalt blue and gilt trim. Mold No 7632. $250.00+.

Plate 87. Bisque double mold of a Japanese couple, 6½". A yes nod is produced from elongated pencil-posts. They are translucent porcelain decorated in subdued tones. A firing crack at the base between their feet has been filled. She has a bamboo fan and he holds a bamboo lidded-basket. $225.00+.

ORIENTALS and BLACK NODDERS...Mix and Match

There was a period of time from 1850 into the early 1900s that similar and almost identical nodders were produced. In that day there was no law to protect copy of designs, thus itinerant workers were free agents. A variety of nodding figurines changed character and personality at the whim of the decorator. Occasionally mold numbers are found, but rarely marks of the manufacturer. Many came from the Saxon district of eastern Germany, the area where clay was found in abundance.

Nodders in this group are bisque and/or glazed porcelain, painted black or white. Some are colorful, others in striking contrast or monotone dress, but distinctively charming.

Plate 88. A four piece jazz band, approximately 4½". Each member of this cosmopolitan group sits on a red cushion and nods a rhythmical no. The American strums a banjo, the English sailor plays a bass violin, the Moroccan is the drummer, and the Turk plays cymbals. The flat-crown straw hat worn by the American musician places this group early 1900. Painted and fired bisque from Germany. $600.00 per set.

Plates 90 and 91. Black mandarin, head nods, tongue wags, hands wave, 6¼". An excellent nodder by Conta and Boehme, unmarked. $450.00+.

Plate 89. Oriental black geisha, 4¼". Seated by an ornate urn, she nods yes and strums her samisen. Unmistakable is her elaborate headdress, flowing robe, and contrasting dark skin. $250.00 – 300.00.

Plate 92. A working black Orientalia supporting a shoulder yoke, 4½". Condition of clothes appears to be a worn faded ocher. A pencil shaped counterweight is incised with mold No. 75 9, 91 B. $160.00 – 185.00.

Plates 93 and 94. Chinese schoolmaster holds his scroll and waves a pointed finger at his pupils. Although one pupil nods yes she also wags her tongue. The other pupil nods with scroll in hand. Two views. $175.00 – 250.00 each.

Plate 95. This serious Chinese schoolmaster is nodding yes, pointing a finger of wisdom, and admonishing his students. His frivolous pupil on the left is sitting cross-legged and agreeably fanning yes, but his problem pupil sits with legs straddled, playing cymbals, and nodding no. 4". $175.00 – 250.00 each.

Plate 96. An aristocratic family, 4¼", 4", and 3". Three color-coordinated yes nodders in subdued tones are highlighted with Pompadour pink and gilt trim. Condition is near mint. The small child's kitten headdress is different. Counterweights are a ball of bisque attached in the neck via a stick. No mark or mold numbers. Left, $225.00. Right, $175.00. Child, $75.00 – 100.00.

Plate 97. A privileged family of five members. Parents are molded together with arms linked. Children include daughter, son, and naughty baby sticking out a loose red tongue. All but the baby nod yes. Gilt emphasizes buttons and trim on the mint green background. Unmarked of German origin. Parents, $225.00. Baby, $50.00. Others, $150.00.

Molds were used over and over by thrifty potters to create interesting personalities. Similarities and differences are depicted in the mix and match section. The period is late 1800s to early 1900.

Plate 98.

Plate 101.

Plate 99.

Plate 102.

Plate 100.

Plate 103.

Plate 104.

Plate 107.

Plate 105.

Plate 108.

Plate 106.

Plate 109.

PARIAN, MORE NODDERS IN THE BISCUIT

In the mid-eighteenth century another form of biscuit porcelain was introduced at the Chateau de Vincennes factory. These figurines did not need the extremely high temperature required to fire porcelain, and lack of glaze improved sharpness of sculpture detail for better quality, especially effective on figurines. This experiment was conducted under Jean Jacques Bachelier, director of the Vincennes studio, later moved to Sevrès.

The English potters Copeland and Garde at Stoke-on-Trent were casting statuettes, some were colorfully decorated. By the nineteenth century successful modeling of biscuit figurines was highly esteemed because they were fired in the kiln once and produced a creamy-white finish that more closely resembled marble than porcelain. The waxy surface was easily cleansed with soap and water. Because of similarity to marble, they called it Parian after the Greek Island of Paros in the Aegean Sea.

Manufactories produced unpainted figurines for colors to be added later, but production of glazed porcelain was never discontinued. Popularity of plain bisque is credited to Bachelier and the French factories.

Plate 110. Another pair of semi-translucent bisque yes nodders, 5½". The chef holds a bird and skillet. His helper has the big wooden spoon. She returned from market with a basket of veggies, pocket purse, and keys still dangling from her waist. Impressed DEP, Mold No. 8381, Mark of Unger, Schneider & Cie, and Carl Schneider's Heirs. Circa 1861 – 1887. $220.00 – 250.00 pair.

Plate 111. The athletic anthropomorphic bear with tennis racket is dressed in people clothes, 6". God given characteristics were portrayed by animals wearing human clothing. Impressed DEP, Mold No. 9884, Mark of Unger, Schneider & Cie, and Carl Schneider's Heirs. Circa 1879 – 1954. $100.00+.

Plate 112. Mary Anning and her friend are a historical pair molded in semi-transparent bisque, 5½". They are an exceptional pair but not of exceptional quality. $325.00 – 350.00 per pair.

The figurine of Mary is molded with her bucket and chisel, the tools of her trade. From research, her nodding companion was Henry Thomas de la Beche who frequently accompanied her on digs, shared her interests, and remained her lifelong friend. Exhibits and records of their findings and those of other early scientists are at the British Museum of Natural History in Piccadilly, and the National Museum of Wales, and also at the Lyme Regis Museum in her home town. Publications chronicle Mary's life work and business that was the sole means of her existence. Impressed marks on the nodding couple DEP (meaning registered). Mold No. 8697 of Unger, Schneider & Cie of Gräfenthal, Thüringia, Germany. Circa 1861–1887.

Mark

Mary Anning, 1799 – 1847

Mary was the daughter of Richard Anning, a cabinetmaker by trade whose hobby was collecting fossils and shells and polishing them for sale to summer tourists. The polished specimens sold in his shop provided additional income, but he was also recognized as one of the earliest collectors and dealers in fossils. Mary lived her entire life at Lyme Regis on the southwest coast of England. Her early pleasure was accompanying her father along the shoreline hunting shells, especially after stormy weather. He taught her to polish those special treasures, a pleasure destined to become her livelihood.

It was after her father died in 1811, when Mary was barely twelve years old, that she attained scientific notice and is credited for discovery of the first specimen of Ichthyosaurus, a streamlined dolphin-like reptile well adapted to marine life. Her most productive digs followed heavy storms after high waves washed the cliffs along the shore. Her discovery of this specimen from earth stratum of the Juriassic Period was unknown at that time and ultimately named Ichthyosarurus.

> Behold, a strange monster our wonder engages!
> If dolphin or lizard your wit may defy.
> Some thirty feet long, on the shore of Lyme Regis
> With a saw for a jaw, and a big staring eye.
> A fish or a lizard? An ichthyosaurus,
> With a big goggle eye, and a very small brain,
> And paddles like mill-wheels in chattering chorus,
> Smiting tremendous the dread-sounding main.
> (From: H.N. Hutchinson. Extinct Monsters, 1893)

Ten years later she found remains of a new saurian, the Plesiosaurus described as a lizard-like reptile with streamlined head, long vertical tail, and small limbs. The Book of Job 40:15–24 mentions a large dinosaur moving a tail like cedar, with bones strong as brass. This creature lived near water 4000 B.C. and was a plant eater.

In 1828, the first time in England, Mary procured the remains of a pterodactyl (Dimotphodon).

Later digs uncovered remains of the Plesiosaurus, plus two large Ichthyosauri, and of a pterodactyl (Dimotphodon). Her discoveries brought the attention of scientists and frequent visitors to the Lyme area. From these findings Charles Darwin developed a theory about evolution of prehistoric living things. Study and selling fossils was Mary's full-time profession and for this she achieved scientific renown. The British Museum of Natural History in Piccadilly exhibits some of her fossils along with her picture and that of her dog, Tray.

Mary never married and died on the 9th of March, 1847 before her 48th birthday. The Lyme Regis Museum in her home town proudly displays her work and honors her achievements. This author has donated Mary Anning and Henry Thomas de la Beche nodders to the Lyme Museum where they are on display.

ICHTHYOSAURUS
A sea mammal

PLESIOSAURUS
A fish lizard

During this period of history, artists such as Francois Boucher and Jean-Antoine Watteau painted scenes of ladies and gentlemen who were trendsetters of their day. Wealth, position, and frivolity enabled the elite to enjoy a luxurious life of leisure.

Delicate expression and artistic talent of French painters is reflected in a fashionable style that set international standards. Nodding figurines in this chapter were molded in bisque porcelain, painted, and fired. Quality workmanship is evident because the original finish today remains quite good. Some credit is attributed to Jean-Jacques Bachelier (1724 – 1806) who believed every decorating detail of porcelain should be perfect, painted but not glazed to obliterate fine detail.

Elegant ladies, dressed in their finest, were depicted as slim, demure, and charming. Their silks came from East India. Much of the ribbon and lace trim was Flemish. Vogue of the day was a chic, tight-fitting bodice with low neckline that frequently emphasized cleavage. A graceful Watteau was trimmed with ruffle pleating or a fly fringe, draped down the back. Waistlines were made to seem narrower with several thicknesses of a fancy wedge-shaped stomacher consisting of stiff, layered, buckram-like material. This constricted style of dress no doubt contributed to ladies' fainting spells. The bodice, sometimes laced, was divided in front to expose an equally decorative underskirt in contrasting colors, an integral part of aristocratic dress. Tight fitting sleeves flared at the elbow with flounces of fancy layered pleats or ruffles. Over the hip was a cumbersome hoop arrangement of drapery called "panier," from the French word meaning basket.

Hair was dusted with wheat or rice meal and either swept into a chignon or fashioned into an elaborate arrangement of curls. Wigs were fashionable for both ladies and gentlemen.

Around milady's neck was a choker-type ribbon or chain necklace suspended with an ornament, called a lavaliere. Duchess de la Vallière (1644 – 1710), who was a mistress of Louis XIV, wore such an ornament. Thus, "lavaliere" has referred to Duchess de la Vallière from that time.

However, it was the talented and powerful Marquise de Pompadour (1721 – 64) who set standards for the Rococo style of the upperclass. Before she became mistress of Louis XV (1710 – 1774), Pompadour was coached for six months on court etiquette. She was a favorite, and together Pompadour and Louis XV shared a lasting mutual interest in the arts. Sculptors, painters, cabinetmakers, engravers, and craftsmen worked in their factory at Sèvres, located a few miles outside Paris. Through Pompadour's influential support and close relationship with the King, Sèvres became the renowned Royal Manufactory. Porcelain was an extravagant luxury and a status symbol, and the royal court demanded mandatory participation. Although the King took other mistresses, Pompadour remained his confidante and enjoyed a life of leisure on the palace grounds the rest of her life.

Nodders and figurines decorated in the famous shade of Rose de Pompadour (sometimes referred as Pompadour pink), have been attributed to Madam's influence and fondness for roses and its use came into prominence under her patronage. A pink ground color with tones of cream, tan, and gold was painted on porcelains at the Sèvres factory as early as 1757. This popular rose-pink ground shade has alternately been attributed to the Comptresse Marie Jeanne Bècu du Barry (1746 – 1793) who, as mistress and successor to Pompadour, was also a patron of the arts. It may be conjecture that this color was associated with either of these royal mistresses because positive proof is lacking. Another theory states the idea possibly originated in England to enhance sales. However, the pleasing rose Pompadour shade is recognized and still in use today.

Gentlemen, as well as ladies wore corsets. Pointed-toe shoes with heels were made of embroidered velvet, silk brocade, or fine leather. The coiffeur was dusted with white meal and fashioned into an intricate style of curls. Elaborate suits of fine fabric were equally resplendent with laces, spangles, and silver and gold embroidered threads. Silk shirts were lavish with ruffles and lace. Collars were replaced with a cravat, a form of jabot around the neck. Front-button breeches were snug and ornately decorated, ending below the knee to meet long white silk stockings held in place with garters. Waistcoats were equally ornate, often decorated with more gold embroidery, covered buttons or buttons of jewels, enamel, and gold. An elegant collarless frock-coat worn over the waistcoat ended near the knee. Pocket flaps were deep and sleeves ended in wide trim or a buttoned cuff.

Many figurines and works of art were produced at Vincennes and later at Sèvres where the factory moved in 1756. Conceivably, the dramatic French style of nodding figurines in this chapter has prompted dealers to suggest, and collectors to believe the nodders are a product of France. Proof to the contrary is stamped on the base of Plate 120. A circle imprint is distinctly marked, "Made in Germany." Lacking further identification, it is the collector's prerogative to decide if other of these nodders are French. Influential French style is evident.

Falconry was the medieval sport of Kings, not to be overlooked among our nodders.

Potteries were numerous in the Austria-Hungary area of central Europe. Plates 115 and 116 are of Teplitz influence. These handsome falconers are from an area where many manufactories were in production around the city of Teplitz. Detail and color are excellent. The falconer does not nod; rather it is the falcon on the man's shoulder that beckons to his call.

Falcons are game birds requiring years of training and persistence. Thus birds will return to their trainer when a bond of affection has been established. Returning crusaders originally carried these birds into Europe from the Middle East and the sport of falconry thus became a popular status symbol.

Plate 113. Young lovers are playing a game of "Bat the Ball" while teasing the pair of frustrated nodding parrots. The tinted rose Pompadour birds are perched on ornamental planters decorated in Rococo style. The raucous bird's gold beaks are open, wings flapping as they strive to intercept the ball. This graceful group typifies the leisure life-style of nobility during the eighteenth century. Milady's playful sporting activity explains the occasion of her mid-calf hemline that is elaborately trimmed with a furbelow flounce, contrasting the floor-length vogue of that day. Mold No. 8664 and 8664 K. 8¾ x 5½". $175.00 – 275.00 per pair.

Plate 114. Imprint marked on the bottom of Plate 120.

Plate 115. Falconer standing beside a planter, 8¾".
The elbogen mark of Conta and Boehme of Pössneck Germany, Thuringia, 1878 – 1937, on base
and mold No. 8587. Same mold no. impressed on
counterweight. $250.00.

The falcon trainer is braced against a tree
stump that is actually a planter with three holes.
(One hole is visible by his right thigh). These holes
were intended for a hanging basket of greenery.
When hung in an open breezeway, the air current
produced a nod of the falcon. The falcon's feet,
pierced with a flat pin, are attached to a bisque
pencil-shaped counterweight to balance the action.

Plate 116. This falconer is braced against a tree
trunk shaped as a candleholder. He is a handsome
youth, elegantly dressed, working his bird and
practicing the technique of his mentor. A stick connects the falcon's feet to the bisque pencil-shaped
counterweight, producing a nod while the bird is
perched on the youth's shoulder, 6½". Artist brush
mark "M." Mold No. 8343 on base of counterweight.
Bisque porcelain. Conta and Boehme of Pössneck,
Germany, Thuringia. 1878–1937. $225.00.

A TABLEAU OF COUPLES

Heads of these attractive young people nod from similar pencil-shaped counterweights
of bisque attached in the neck via a stick, with one exception. The counterweight of the
lady in Plate 117 is original, but unusual. It is bisque and pencil-shaped, but connected to
the neck with a piece of horn rather than the ordinary stick of wood. These bisque porcelain groups are richly painted in subtle hues. They are yes nodders.

Plate 117. A pair of chess players seated on an ottoman, a high-back cushioned sofa with rounded arms, elevated on a Rococo base. 5¼" x 5¼". Semi-translucent bisque. Mold No. 8610 (man), 7577 (lady). The lady's Pompadour style bodice with a square low neckline complements the gold lavaliere at her throat. A chessboard rests on the gold pedestal table. Four chessmen are on the board, two have been removed, and another is in the lady's right hand. This group is a chimney piece because the plain sofa back is completely void of color. $275.00+.

Plate 118. Teenagers seated on cushioned stools. 5" x 5½". Mold No. 8610 K impressed on the posts. The table is covered with an elegant embroidered cloth edged with fringe trim. Chessmen on the chessboard are scattered across the table. The girl's overskirt, or polonaise, is caught up in puffs and then drawn back to show her ruffled petticoat. The back side of this nodder is well defined. $275.00+.

Plate 119. Two couples and four nodding heads are playing a card game. Yes, they are using actual playing cards. 6½" x 8¼". Mold No. 8587 on all weights. $450.00 – 550.00.

Plate 120. "The Old, Old Story," 5½", is another chimney piece. A pair of lovers are seated on an ottoman. With one arm embracing his charming companion, he gently holds her hand as if poised to ask a question. A strand of pearls at her throat and the low square neckline are concealed behind her large fan. $250.00+.

Plate 121. The chamber musicians are mounted on a Rococo base. 6½" x 5". Mold No. 7568 (man), 7577 (lady). The lady wears a gold lavaliere. Seated on a four-legged stool, she accompanies her handsome cavalier on the harpsichord. An army wife purchased this set at a street market in the 1940s while her husband was serving a tour of duty in Germany. $275.00+.

Plate 122. An Oriental pastime, fanning a butterfly. 6¾". Bisque in the rococo style. The Chinaman rests on a large fancy shell designed as a planter studded with coralene beading. His queue curls around his right shoulder. Only the fan in his left hand waves. This is one of a pair, his missing partner sits on a matching shell and also fans a butterfly. $95.00.

The popularity of England's beloved Queen Victoria (1837 – 1901) characterizes an era known as Victorian. Its profound influence on architecture, furnishings, and decor lasted into the twentieth century.

The Meissen factory at Albrechtsburg was first to perfect the manufacture of porcelain and the chinoiserie style of their work reflected Chinese influence. Other factories subsequently began production throughout the continent and copied from Meissen and Sèvres. Skilled workers sworn to secrecy of this zealously guarded mystery were unscrupulous and migrated from factory to factory. The secret of porcelain was no longer secret.

The eighteenth century brought revolutionary, political and social change, much of it due to Napoleon's influential rise to power. This established a new class of people with innovative ideas and neoteric resources. Napoleon's trade barrier between England and the continent benefitted the Balkan countries which in turn inspired German manufactories to produce Middle Eastern type nodders.

Figurines became increasingly popular throughout Europe, but because of rarity and cost were mostly available to aristocrats and the wealthy upper classes.

Dawn of the Victorian era brought new demands that stimulated craftsmen and potters to produce artifacts in quantity. Nodders became available to a new buying public privileged to spend money on objects of art and luxury. To remain productive and justify cost, factories manufactured cheaper quality products that

Plates 123 and 124. Early porcelain inkwell, 3½" x 4". Sultan and sultana nod, sitting on ornate cushions with their magic oil lamp between them. Old inkwells had an inset container for the ink. A quill pen, carefully pointed for writing was dipped in the inkwell. The other jar had many tiny holes at the top and was the blotter. This held powdered sandarac that was sprinkled on wet ink to hasten drying. A substance like fine sand, it was a powdered resin from the large pinaceous tree of Morocco. Ben Franklin signed the Declaration of Independence with such a pen. Similar desk accouterments were popular in early 1800, but this nodding couple atop an inkwell are rare. No price available.

appealed to the purse of a new market, the affluent bourgeoisie as well as the working class. The new buying public seemed well pleased. Creative modelers produced some of the charming nodders we occasionally find today.

Animated nativity figurines were known as early as the sixteenth century, but to the Victorians, figurines with movable parts were novel fascination. Of course, this was the nineteenth century before flicks, radio, and television. The traveling circus, or a hurdy-gurdy man grinding an organ with his playful little monkey provided amusement. Nodding figurines were unique.

The nodder was entertainment for every age. The nodder could charm and distract the sick and the shut-in. A small child's play-game could be to beat the sandman before the nodding ceased.

Many nodders were modeled in bisque and reflect people's everyday lifestyle. They were diversified. Some depicted actual personages. Some were sophisticated. Some were comical. Some were tawdry. Some were made in pairs. Some were animals. The majority had one movable part. Others had several. All were charming.

Most nodders in this chapter nod yes, unless otherwise noted and are of German manufacture.

Plate 125. A pair of Arabian post nodders sitting with legs crossed at the ankle, 4". Plain bisque, except for glazed cobalt trim and gilt accent. Silk was comfortable in their hot climate and the loose drawstring drawers were girded at the waist with a voluminous sash. The headdress is a handkerchief fastened with a band. Her headdress has a side drape, and she also holds an open fan. Near mint condition with artist brush marks. $275.00+.

Plate 126. This Arabian pair nods no, 3½". Translucent porcelain, near mint condition. A Chicago gallery acquired props from several movie sets. According to their records the sultan was used on the set in *Camille*, starring Greta Garbo and Robert Taylor. The couple sits on cushions with bare feet and legs crossed. The sultana's head wrap conceals her hair, but large earrings are prominent. The sultan has heavy brows, a full dark beard, and jewelry at his neck. Their gesturing arms and hands do not move but are molded with the body, rarely seen on nodders, especially in such excellent condition. $275.00+.

Plate 127. Turkish sultan and sultana, 3¼". Plain bisque porcelain, Pompadour pink highlights, and gilt beading. Turbans are long pieces of cloth wrapped around skull caps. Her gold headband complements his gold button adornments. Great nodders, although sultana's counterweight is not original. Mold No. 521349 on both. $350.00 pair.

Plate 128. This couple is richly dressed in silk studded with coralene beads and tasseled fezzes, 3". No marks. Mint condition. Translucent bisque. His mustache resembles Turk figurines modeled by Kaendler in the eighteenth century. His eyes and brows are more slanted than hers. Pear shaped bisque counterweights are attached in the neck via a stick. $350.00 pair.

Plate 129. Interesting comparison of four bisque and porcelain nodders in Mid-Eastern dress holding open fans. Caucasoid features, wavy hair, and wrapped turbans with side drape. Sizes range from 3½" to 5". (These nodders are also found as pairs.) $100.00 – 150.00 each.

Plate 130. An Indian mahout, spear in hand, is intent on his prey. Elephant's head moves up and down and drifts from side to side. Counterweight inside the elephant body is bisque and not removable, 4¾". Bisque porcelain of translucent quality. $220.00.

Plate 131. Blackamoor with his long pole, 3". Painted pewter nodder in worn condition. Circa 1880. A steel spring strap connects the shaking head to the body cavity. Moors lost most of their land to Spain during the Middle Ages. Refugees resettled in North Africa and today are of Muslim, Jewish, or Turkish descent. It is a misconception that Moors are black. The idea stems from William Shakespeare's *Othello*. Early in the eighteenth century Blackamoors were popular subjects for the modeler and frequently depicted as footmen. $250.00+.

Plate 132. Dickensian Man, 3½". Blue under-glaze anchor mark of Ernst Bohne Söhne, a factory in the area of Thuringia, Germany. Circa 1878 – 1920. $145.00.

Tales from Charles Dickens (1812 – 1870) and his remarkable characters inspired artists. Bohne's characterization of the Dickensian man makes this an interesting nodder in seventeenth century dress. He is seated in a chair with dour expression and blush cheeks. A tri-corner hat covers much of his powdered curly wig. Shirt sleeves are ruffled at the cuff, his vest is buttoned around his corpulent body, and over all this is a long coat. His deep blue eyes match the color of his knee breeches that meet stockings below his knees. Low-cut slippers complete his seventeenth century dress.

Plate 133. This dour faced little man is nodding in his chair. He wears gold rim glasses and holds an unidentified object in his left hand. Translucent bisque. Mold No. 5479. Germany. $125.00.

Plate 134. This is a comical puzzle. But he couldn't be happier wearing his long pink nightgown with a crushed hat on his head and shoes on his feet. He appears to be sitting on a chamber pot and he nods vigorously. $145.00+.

Plates 137 and 138. Colonial gentleman with an umbrella under his arm and sack over his shoulder, 7½". Animal with restored ears not identified. With a raised hand he nods and talks. The wired jaw moves his tongue and goateed chin in a realistic greeting. On the base a partial blue ink stamp is unidentified. Probably late 1800s. Germany. $220.00.

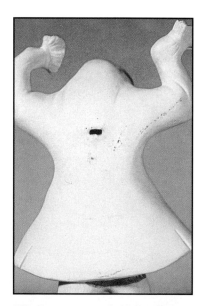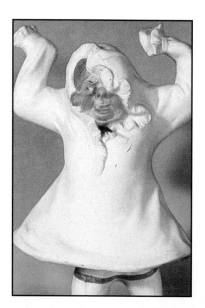

Plates 135 and 136. What a struggle to get into-or-out-of that nightshirt. 7½". A whimsical (wo)man(?) in excellent condition. A visible wire under her/his chin is thrust through the bisque body to enhance lively swaying motion. Unusual. $195.00.

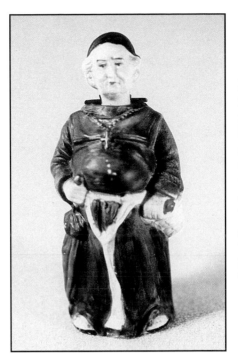

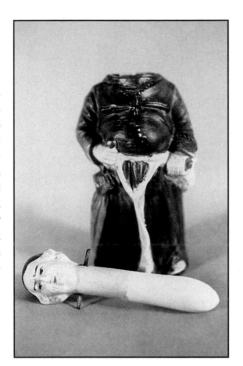

Plate 139 and 140. The pot-bellied friar with a stern expression is a man of the cloth. Translucent bisque porcelain. 5½". His habit is girdled with a knotted rope, sandals on his feet, carrying a red umbrella and basket of fruit. He is a post nodder with flat neck pin that does not rest in shoulder grooves. Consequently his head can turn any direction. "GERMANY" is imprinted at the base. Late nineteenth century. $140.00+.

Plates 141 and 142. Two monks wearing gray habits are in charge of the establishment. One monk works in the winery, the other is also keeper of the keys. Rosaries are worn under the apron when they are working. The friar in the brown habit has come to sample libation and extends a greeting. Many of the world's finest wines were produced within the cold stone walls of a monastery. Good food and spirits sustained their austere life. Front and back views show several wine containers. These three nodders, 5½", have a thin wire from the side collar through the neck so the nodding head is not removable. Mold numbers 7105, 7106, and 7108. Germany. Late nineteenth century. $150.00+ each.

Plates 143 and 144. A bald Augustinian monk, 9". This two-way swayer is highly glazed terracotta except for head, hands, and sandaled feet. He seems in a pensive mood. Or is it penitent? His rosary hangs from the cincture tied around his waist. Product of Portugal. Circa 1900. $150.00.

Plates 145 and 146. Jewish man swaying and holding a red cloth in his hands. Portugal. Early 1900. $150.00.

Plate 147. Policeman drawing his saber and also wearing a holster and gun. Two-way swayer. 9¼". Mold No 710. Product of Portugal. Early 1900. $100.00 – 150.00.

Plate 149. A country woman with a pitcher. One of a pair, mate is missing. $175.00.

CHIMNEY PIECES, CABINET PIECES, FLAT-BACKS

The nodder with a plain undecorated back side was intended for front viewing, sometimes referred to as a flat-back, chimney, shelf, cabinet, or mantle piece. They were popular bric-a-brac in the Victorian parlor and affordable to the pocketbook. Likewise, the manufacturer was pleased because a partially painted figurine reduced production cost.

Plate 148. The weight lifter, 5½". From a squatting position he is straining to hoist those barbells and perspiration is running down his forehead and cheek. Painted and fired bisque. Early 1900s. Germany. $225.00.

Nodding chimney pieces were manufactured in bisque, in glazed porcelain with gilt highlights, with colorful decoration, and sometimes splashed coralene beading. Elaborate nodders were products of better manufactories and fine condition is evident today if you are fortunate to find them. A characteristic of Victorian nodders is the flat metal pin wedged through the neck. Often the aperture was grooved to accommodate the neck pin, but not always.

Curio cabinets and what-not shelves were necessary to display this new bric-a-brac and provided additional work for craftsmen. Small novelties were required to fill these shelves and our charming nodders played an important part.

Historical and fictional figurines were molded but generally overlooked among nodders. However the nodding genre characters depicted daily lifestyle and humor of the people.

Victorian nodders frequently wear floor-length garments, toes barely protruding, such as Plate 157. This was a distinguishing trait of Kate Greenway's people, for it seems she had a problem drawing feet. If this idea belonged to Greenway, it was copied by other modelers and no laws at that time protected a copyright.

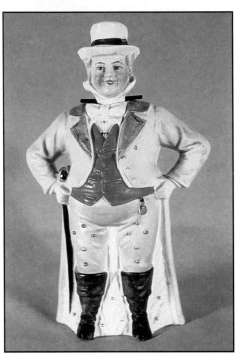
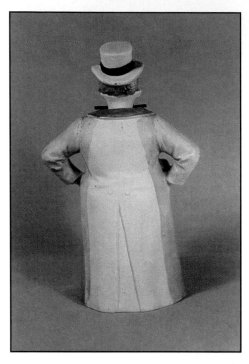

Plate 150 and 151. A pleasing translucent bisque post nodder, 7½". Impeccably attired in a cut-away coat, vest, and buttoned shirt, he is indeed a handsome fellow. His hair is trimmed to accommodate the high shirt collar and silk cravat tied under his chin. Tight breeches meet leather boots below his knees. With a beaver hat, gold handled walking stick, and pocket watch dangling from his vest, he is quite a dandy. $250.00+.

Plate 152 and 153. A jilted suitor, 6¾". A good post nodder with a bisque head and translucent porcelain body. Near mint condition. The hat brim shades his bespectacled blue eyes. He is meticulously dressed in a long coat, vest, shirt, and prominent bow tie. The coat separates his ample belly, exposing a gold watch and chain. Breeches and polished leather boots meet below the knee. A flat pin rests on smooth shoulders permitting his head to turn any direction and better watch for his paramour. His glare in the distance and downturned mouth are added amusement because he sits with arms akimbo holding a drooping bouquet and walking stick. His lady fair has not appeared at the appointed hour. $250.00+.

Plate 154 and 155. Two ladies relaxing in rocking chairs with their pipes. 4½" x 4¼". Good quality semi-translucent porcelain, glazed inside. Mobcap worn over a hairdo pulled in a bun at the back. $150.00 – 200.00.

Plate 156. A proper Victorian lady is relaxed in her chair, nodding and enjoying high tea, 6¾". Mold No 7642. Painted and fired bisque and decorated with gold beading. $275.00 – 375.00.

Plate 157 and 158. A charming blue-eyed blonde girl with lovely doll face, 6¾". Bisque. Her coat with cape collar and matching hat have a dark luster fur trim. The cat under her arm has a red ribbon around its neck. Her young male companion is missing. $145.00+.

Plate 159. Victorian lady wearing a Japanese style kimono, pale blue accents are enhanced with brown luster trim, 4½". She is one of a pair, mate missing. $125.00.

PAIRS

Charming nodders in this section depict everyday activity of the bourgeois and working class. Pairs are especially pleasing but increasingly rare. They are of European origin and some are chimney pieces painted and fired in the biscuit.

Additional nodding pairs are found in the Chapter, Something Else.

Plate 161. Dutch barge captain with his lunch pail is walking with his wife who is also carrying a broom. There is no groove in the shoulder aperture so heads can turn and talk. 7½". Semi-translucent porcelain glaze. $275.00 – 350.00 pair.

Apparently wives and brooms had special meaning. According to folklore, the German wife who swept a circle around her husband kept him eternally true. Maybe that is why a broom was so handy.

Plate 160. An interesting couple, 6½". The boot polisher, perhaps a stable hand, wears a jockey cap. His wife is wearing an apron and holding a broom. Translucent bisque. $275.00 – 350.00 pair.

Plate 162. Marital discord in the bedroom? 7". Dressed in their night clothes, are they going to bed angry or getting up that way? Semi-translucent glazed porcelain. $275.00 – 350.00 pair.

Plate 163. More German humor, "I Never feel Dry," 6½". Head of this nodder matches the argumentative wife's head in Plate 162. $100.00.

Plate 165. Old salt carried his big bottle home and the little woman met him with a pitcher, 7¼". $250.00 – 350.00 per pair.

Plate 164. Old salt with a pot belly and his buxom wife, 5½". He is painted on the back side, she is not. A ruffled scarf is wrapped around her shoulders across the front of her bosom. This translucent bisque couple are seen in several sizes. $275.00 – 350.00 pair.

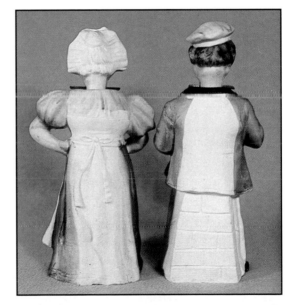

Plate 166 and 167. Tavern proprietors, front and rear views, 7½". Bisque. Artist brush marks. This industrious couple, with red nose and rosy cheeks are on break. He enjoys a cigar and foaming tankard of beer as she drinks a cup of tea. They are translucent bisque post nodders with a flat pin piercing the neck. The shoulder aperture is not grooved, permitting them to face each other, nod, and chat. $275.00 – 350.00 pair.

Plate 168. Children in bisque porcelain, 5". Repaired. Artist brush marks. German. $250.00 – 350.00 pair.

Two proper young people are seated on upholstered chairs. Brother reads to sister who is knitting a stocking. Her cape is tied with a big polka-dot bow. Their warm coats are floor length. No wire-rim glasses here, but visible holes at the temples were intended for glasses. These Staffordshire-type nodders are bisque and have been painted and fired sans heavy glaze.

STAFFORDSHIRE-TYPE NODDERS

During the nineteenth century a form of peasant art was prevalent in the Staffordshire district of England. Workmanship was of good quality but artistic creativity was lacking. Although not considered great objects of art by connoisseurs, the figurines are popular collectibles.

Factories copied style, detail, and technique. Whereas the German economy was depressed, many Victorian nodders were manufactured on the continent and marketed throughout England. These Staffordshire-types are hard-paste and often referred to as Staffordshire, an inexpensive substitute. Thus today we frequently find pleasing Staffordshire-type figurines in the markets and they are quite collectible.

Collectors have been led to believe nodders such as these were made in the Staffordshire district of England and con-

Plate 169. Glazed Staffordshire-type pair. This exemplifies duplication of popular molds used by thrifty Victorian manufacturers. $240.00 – 350.00 per pair.

fuse them with Staffordshire. An actual maker is seldom identified. At this writing I dispute the Staffordshire nomenclature and refer to the travel experience of my good friends, Ted and Marty Quell, of Lathrup Village, Michigan. Quell has a number of fine nodders in his collection. On a tour of London in May 1987, the Quells made a train trip to Stoke-on-Trent, and I quote Ted.

"This is a center of the Staffordshire district where we had been led to believe many porcelain nodder pairs were made during Victorian times. There were many factories at this point, but we were advised to go on to Henley, about ten miles to the north where there was a large museum of bisque, porcelain, terracotta, etc...a lady who had been in charge of the porcelain section of this immense museum for more than 20 years told me that nodders were never made in the Staffordshire district, but that antique dealers labeled them Staffordshire because this magic word connoted quality pieces."

Further discussion with dealers concerning the origin of so-called Staffordshire nodders corroborates Quell's findings. I am in agreement with their knowledge and judgment and believe the composition of these nodders is hard-paste and that they were made in Germany. These comments were also concurred by an Englishman who is a frequent patron of the London antique markets. He believes nodders he sees and collects on the English street markets are not of English origin. Therefore, I refer to them as Staffordshire-type. Granted, they closely resemble their English Staffordshire counterparts, but they are German hard-paste. During a heyday of the Victorian period, the Staffordshire name elicited an acceptable and inexpensive export to the American public. Conceivably, comparable heavy glaze and basic white color has erroneously convinced collectors of an English origin.

Whatever the origin of these nodders, they intrigue the collector. Like other artifacts at that time, they lack marks of identification. Personalities and animals were popular subjects. We find children in pairs, sitting, standing, holding pets and objects, in costumes or dress of the day. Some wear wire-rim glasses. If holes are at the temples, with no wire-rims, glasses may have been removed, or were never there.

Our nodding figurines resemble their English Staffordshire counterparts, the glaze, color, detail, and gilt trim. (The gilt trim on Staffordshire-type nodders further indicates German origin.) They are not of finest quality because heavy glaze minimized features. Most of the Staffordshire-types I have seen are post nodders. The original flat pin rather than a round one

through the neck typifies the Victorian era.

Staffordshire-type nodders are found in pairs. If a mate is missing, it could have been separated at the time of sale, later, or through breakage and careless handling. However, some were designed as singles. Because our nodders are unmarked and perform in silence, they provide no clue to their background or history. An additional feature of the Staffordshire-type nodder is the plain back side discussed in this chapter.

With increasing value, collectors today appraise Staffordshire as a popular and desirable collectible. Escalating prices would most certainly have delighted Victorian potters.

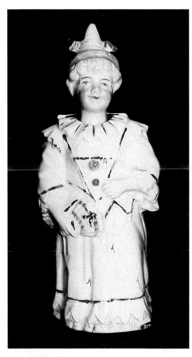

Plate 170. Smiling blonde girl wearing a floor length clown dress and pointed hat, 7¼". This type figurine will be seen with heavy glazing throughout. Circa 1890 – 1900. Germany. $175.00.

Plate 171. A proud blond boy dressed in a clown suit with cobalt blue accents, 7". His puppet doll has a stick handle. $175.00.

Plate 172 and 173. A young barrister wearing wire-rim glasses, 6¾". White robe, books, and quill pen are enhanced with gilding. The white wig covers most of her golden hair. Counterweight, pictured, is unusual for a Staffordshire-type nodder. $300.00.

Plate 174. "Three o'clock in the morning" is a fairing. No movement here. 3¼" x 3¼". Circa 1860 – 1890. Excellent condition. Another close resemblance to English Staffordshire and Staffordshire-types is this frozen fairing. It is a heavily glazed, brightly colored figurine and deserves mention. Impressed elbogen mark of Conta & Boehme. Germany. $125.00.

These fairings were an inexpensive souvenir, won or sold at a fair or sometimes on the streets for a pittance. Such occasions created an aura of fun and excitement, excuse for a holiday, and the latest news and gossip of the day. Like our nodders, the fairing was in abundant supply from German factories, and many of the fairings were marked.

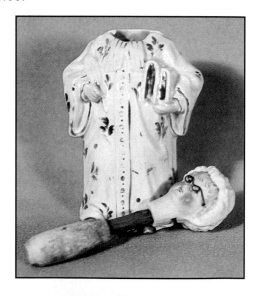

Plate 175. Elbogen mark.

CHIMNEY PIECES
Staffordshire-type

Brush marks or mold numbers on nodders are not meaningful to the collector. Sometimes the artist tested the bottom or inside of a figurine with several brush strokes before decorating.

Many nodders of Victorian vintage are frequently damaged and/or have evidence of restoration. Mint specimens are no longer common. Near mint condition is a fortunate find. Sadly lacking is identifiable marks of individual potters. Nor are mold numbers a matter of record, but if chronicled would aid our research.

Plate 176. A pair of well-dressed children, 7". Post nodders. $240.00 – 325.00 per pair.

This highly glazed blue-eyed blond couple wear wire-rim glasses and are dressed as adults. The girl's gathered cape is secured with a bow at her neck. One hand grasps ruffled folds of the cape as if to prevent dragging on the street. A ribbon fastens the ruffled bonnet under her chin. A pet pug snuggles under her arm. Victorian children were frequently modeled with their pets, toys, and other objects.

Her chubby companion wears a floor length cutaway coat. The cut of his four-button vest exposes his ruffled shirt and large cravat. Fancy knee breeches meet stockings below his knee. One hand clasps a bell, the other holds a walking stick. His top hat appears to have fancy trim at the hairline but is actually a second cap worn under his top hat.

Plate 177. Two brothers, 7". The one holds a slice of watermelon, the other a bell and walking stick. Dress (similar to the lad in Plate 176) but highlighted with cobalt decoration. Post nodders. $150.00 each.

Plate 178. Two children nod in rhythm holding string instruments, 5". These fair-haired youngsters with rosy cheeks and a serious expression are playing music, seated in comfortable armchairs. The girl strums an auto-harp, the boy a lute. They wear fancy hats and wire-rim glasses. Flowers on the girl's skirt complement the boy's knee breeches, matching striped stockings and slippers. $200.00 – 225.00 pair.

These nodders are usually fair-haired, blue-eyed, and frequently with wire-rim glasses. Inside body and post counterweights are highly glazed.

Plate 179. A pair of pets, the bulldog with brown spots and a perky Siamese cat, 5½". Both in excellent condition. $325.00+ each.

Victorians loved animals. The dog and cat sit upright on the cushions of elegant rococo armchairs. The smooth-haired dog's neck collar is accented with cobalt. Gray to black distinguishes the green-eyed cat's markings with the tail curled around its feet. Although heads of both animals nod on a short post, the modeler's skill is evident because cat and dog perform well.

During the eighteenth century Chinese sculptors were known as people face-makers. Commissioned artists were capable of reproducing remarkable likenesses in an unusual art form, significant because of its excellent realism. This could be in the form of a bust, often life-size, or a realistic scaled-down effigy, more miniature in size but portrayed as full-length statuettes like our one-of-a-kind mandarin and his lady in Plate 180. They were real people, but neither their name nor that of the sculptor is recorded.

Portraits of notables and holy men were painted on canvas, or the likeness was carved in wood and stone. But during this century talented Chinese potters invaded the artists' workshops and honed their modeling skills, using only their hands, some clay, and a few tools. They were clay modelers, the face-makers of their day.

Mandarins were high officials in Imperial China with a powerful status and close association with their emperor, the "Son of Heaven." They were administra-

Plate 181

tors of the emperor's realm and their prestige and authority was second only to that of the emperor. A jewel on the mandarin's hat, denoting his rank, is now missing.

These full-figured statuettes were real people molded in miniature. View of the backside, Plate 181, shows the couple seated on barrel-form garden seats. Posed in the prime of life, they are proportioned to scale, attired in everyday clothes for conducting official duties. Now, two centuries later, their condition is no longer pristine.

Birds, scrolls, clouds, and the four-clawed dragon chasing a flaming pearl are lavishly embroidered on the rich yellow-gold background of the mandarin's silk robe. The backside is mostly plain. One flowing sleeve turned up at the cuff reveals an unidentified object in his hand. The pointed "hoof" cuff conceals his other hand. Manchus were renowned as skilled horsemen. Thus his robe has the necessary center slit for straddling his horse.

Plate 180

Facial features detail the mandarin's slanted eyelids, focused eyes, distinct nostrils, and ears. A long queue of human hair is braided down his back (a compulsory Manchu rule). On one foot is a thick wooden platform slipper with upturned toe. The other foot is missing. These statuettes are mounted on painted hewn boards. There is evidence of repair, especially around the aperture where damage frequently occurs.

The lady's refined features are comparably distinct. Jewels on her ears are now missing. Hair is meticulously groomed and styled with ornaments. Her iron-red silk robe, also embroidered, has full flowing sleeves concealing her hands in her lap. A trim black border outlines the pleated skirt, barely revealing tips of her dainty shoes.

Clay forms such as these were molded around a wooden armature and sculpted in terra-cotta clay, hardened and then painted with oils. Occasionally head coverings, and sometimes the coiffure, was detachable. However, because our couple are nodding figurines, the entire heads can be removed from the body cavity, as illustrated in Plate 182. A neck pin was not used here in the manner of later nodding figurines. Rather, both heads are well balanced on the tightly wrapped bamboo stick suspended in the neck and counterbalanced with a weight. Head movement can be described as a slow rolling motion with a slight nod.

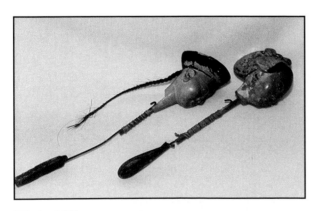

Plate 182

This form of art was in use for about a century, a skill possibly handed down by members of the same family. Today it is rare, and rarely seen. Effigies of notables are in private collections and on display in museums today.

Some chronology

A coarse, heavy china was known during the Han dynasty (206 B.C. to 220 A.D.) and history attributes this technique and its use to the Chinese.

As early as the eleventh century an important imperial porcelain manufactory was in operation at Ching-tê-Chên on the left bank of the Ch'ang River in northern Kiangsi Province. Nearby rich mineral deposits provided the nucleus for ceramic production, an industry destined for world renown.

By the thirteenth century, Marco Polo's travels to the Far East introduced china to Europe. Conceivably, some figurines with separate parts were among these treasures. Other historians relate knowledge of articulated figurines to the travels of Vasco de Gama. He sailed around the Cape of Good Hope and opened trade in the Far East, returning to Europe with many curiosities. Ships left Europe in late winter and with good fortune sailed homeward prior to the monsoon season the following year.

In 1602 the East India Company established seaport trade at Canton (now Guangzhou) by approval of Chinese Emperor K'ang Hsi. Cargo was transferred between junks and sailing ships anchored at Whampoa, then traveled from Macau up the Pearl River for trading at Canton. During this interim the mariners, "foreign devils," were confined to hongs in rows of white buildings within a square mile area. Daily activity of the Chinese could be observed from this vantage point but living conditions were "crammed together like sweet meat jars in a box of bran" void of outhouses and a back door. Women were not permitted. Foreigners were forbidden to speak the Chinese language, or the Chinese to speak a foreign language. A limited six month trading period was conducted in pidgin English through intermediaries.

In the seventeenth and eighteenth centuries numerous potteries produced fine porcelain at Tè-hua in the Fukien province, an area about 100 miles south of Chien-yang known for pure white porcelain with a lovely luster called blanc de chine. Some figurines made at Tê-hua were said to have detachable heads and hands. This leads us to believe some modeling was in the form of a nodder.

Early in the seventeenth century significant information surfaced in Europe through letters from a Jesuit missionary, Père d'Entrecolles. This priest observed as he traveled throughout this porcelain manufacturing center. His letters mentioned two ingredients, kaolin and a finely powdered granite called petuntse. Using clear mountain water from the nearby Chang River was convenient for refining the clay. Fused together, the hard glassy surface became porcelain. His description of craftsmen in mass production on an assembly line, each performing and perfecting a single task, is likened to Henry Ford's innovative assembly of the Model-T Ford early this century.

The hub of this production was Ching-tê-Chên, a densely populated industrial city known for skilled potters and incessant fires from thousands of working kilns that perpetuated a daytime haze and nighttime glow. (see page 70)

In verse, Henry Wadsworth Longfellow (1807 – 1882) reflected back to his youth and the impressionable visits with an old potter in his Portland, Maine, boyhood home. A few years prior to his death Longfellow wrote *Keramos*, a lengthy ode to potters. Musical refrain extols the work of modelers around the world and this excerpt is descriptive of the town of Ching-tê-Chên.

"O'er desert sands, o'er gulf and bay,
O'er Ganges and o'er Himalay,
Bird-like I fly, and flying sing,
To flowery kingdoms of Cathay,
And bird-like poise on balanced wing
Above the town of King-tê-ching,
A burning town, or seeming so,—
Three thousand furnaces that glow
Incessantly, and fill the air
With smoke uprising, gyre on gyre,
And painted by the lurid glare,
Of jets and flashes of red fire."

China reserved her finest pieces for the emperor and courts so the export items produced in quantity were considered inferior. She resisted change, but China's profound influence on the art world is highly esteemed and many fine specimens are in museums and private collections.

CHINESE NODDERS

Plate 183. Chinese gentleman and his lady nod yes, 4½". They are brightly decorated bisque and their ruffled collars are more unusual. A colorful bird is painted on the lady's open fan and the gentleman rests a long opium pipe on his ankle. The small hole in one hand probably held a missing umbrella. Early 1900s. Germany. $200.00 – 250.00 pair.

Plate 184. Seated mandarin of high cultural standing, 4½". Painted and fired bisque. No marks. $125.00.

Plate 185. Chinese jester with his tools, the gold teapot and his big feather fan, 3¾". His dress, his pointed headdress, and his makeup complete his appearance. His loose tongue is part of his act. Porcelain from China. $75.00 – 125.00.

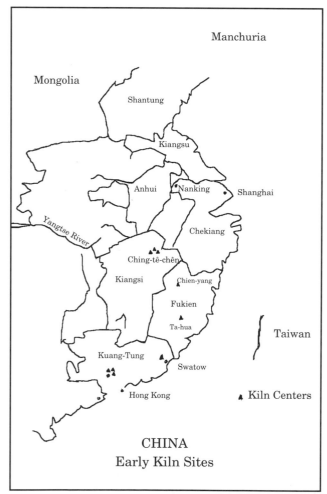

CHINA
Early Kiln Sites

(Map labels: Manchuria, Mongolia, Shantung, Kiangsu, Anhui, Nanking, Shanghai, Yangtse River, Chekiang, Ching-tê-chên, Kiangsi, Chien-yang, Fukien, Ta-hua, Taiwan, Kuang-Tung, Swatow, Hong Kong, ▲ Kiln Centers)

Plate 186. Chinese jester in a brilliant red robe is holding tools of his trade, 6¼". Fired and glazed clay. Motion is activated from a spring inside the body. Purchased at Narita Airport, 1987. $15.00 – 20.00.

Documenting the background of nodders is problematic. Lacking research, Grace Chu (co-author of *Oriental Antiques and Collectibles, a Guide,* by Arthur and Grace Chu), agrees there is a vast void in our knowledge. In Chu's opinion, Europeans as well as Japanese copied from the Chinese who were masters of technique, and their work substantiates this fact. Once the Chinese made something, according to Chu, they did not allow the art to die. This is evidenced by reappearance of nodding-type figurines seen today, ink-stamped and labeled "Made in China."

Plates 187 and 188. Front and back view of four ceramic nodders from China. The scholar on the right led the priest on the left, along with the monkey and pig to Southeast Asia in search of the sutras (sacred sermons of Buddha). There they found writings and returned with them to China. The pig and monkey are featured as anthropomorphic. Circa 1981. No price available.

Plate 189. Smiling Chinese boy with bobbing head and folded hands, 6½". Molded in clay and painted. Purchased in San Francisco Chinatown, July 1992. Paper label "Made in China." $20.00.

Plate 190. The owner of an antique shop in Hawaii called this Chinese couple garden figures. They are heavily glazed porcelain, 4½". Apparently a position of third rank was intended by the modeler as evidenced by an embedded blue "sapphire" on their headdress. They nod no from the small extension of his goatee and her double chin. Ink stamped, "Made in China." (The pair and singles have also appeared in the London flea markets and junk shops in the States.) $50.00.

Visions of Chinese culture bring to mind centuries of magnificent art work, fine porcelains, lacquer, carved jade and ivory, luxurious silks, and delicate embroidery. However, peasants from rural areas and small communities were no less talented, so their culture was expressed in other handicrafts which was their kind of folk art. Some of the Chinese nodders depicted in this section are believed to be products of China, dating from the late nineteenth and early twentieth centuries. Composition and glaze indicates they were probably products of southern China and known as Canton ware. They characterize style and activities of the plebeian peoples.

These are yes nodders unless otherwise indicated.

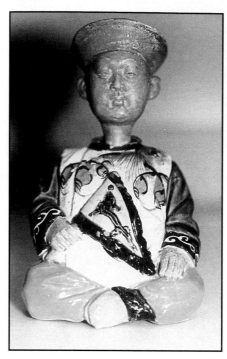

Plates 191 and 192. Two views of a seated Chinese man, 5¼". Unglazed face and hands. A long braided black queue can be seen from under his hat. His crab claw crackle-glaze tunic is also decorated with crabs. Design of the three-cornered banner in his right hand is an archaic dragon, symbol of guardianship. Solid base. Good nodding action produced from the bell-shaped lead counterweight. Terra-cotta composition. Circa 1870s. $175.00+.

Plate 193. A grotesque grinning Chinaman with drooping mustache, sallow skin, pendulous ears, giddy expression, and a long queue hanging down his back, 3¾". This fragile chalkware nodder, still in fair condition, was made from a gypsum compound and then painted with oils. Solid base. Flower-pot shaped lead counterweight. A rare nineteenth century nodder from the Qing dynasty (1644 – 1911). $200.00.

Plates 194 and 195. Terra-cotta nodding Chinese peasant with jar of spices and stick in each hand, 3¼". The apron embellished with an emblem covers the front of her crab claw, crackle-glaze garment. Turban-like head wrap has animalistic fastening. The head nods from the bell-shaped lead counterweight. Worn condition is not unusual for this type of nodder. $125.00+.

Plate 196. The old Chinaman is a mud man perched on a rocky base. His loose tongue and outstretched arm appear to chase the goose from a fish he holds in his left hand, 5¼" x 6¼". Chinese elders are revered as older and wiser, thus their features depict qualities of wisdom and serenity. Mark: CHINA, plus a triangle of Chinese characters. 1920 – 1940. $200.00.

Mud figures such as this old fisherman were reddish-gray clay, richly glazed except for exposed body parts. These figurines were inexpensive, used in planters and aquariums depicting working class Chinese peasants. Early mud figures are popular collectibles and have increased in value. Newer mud figures on today's market are in the $25.00 to $50.00 range, but lack the distinction of earlier ones.

JAPANESE NODDERS

Nodders and numerous other art objects were manufactured for export to Europe and carried to the States by travelers and missionaries. Lack of identification concludes that many early figurines predate 1890 (refer to the McKinley Tariff Act in Construction of Nodders). I believe some Oriental nodders in this section are from the latter part of the last century.

Many date from the Meiji period (1867 – 1912) when Japan's gateway was opened to the Western world. The cultural arts of Japan, China, and Korea are closely aligned, however inherent characteristic talents of Japanese craftsman are distinguishable. Their skilled artisans were innately aggressive perfectionists and renowned copiers as previously discussed.

They nod yes unless otherwise indicated.

Plate 197. An antique and rare triple terra-cotta mold of a musical Japanese family, 3½" x 5¾". The poised kimono-clad mother strums her samisen with a plectrum, little daughter beats a drum while father holds his bamboo instrument. This family is of high standing and enjoy the good life. Three nodding heads, original metal counterweights, but in worn condition, circa 1890. $250.00 – 300.00.

Plate 198. Austere Japanese gentleman sits with feet crossed, holding a large fan, 6½". His white flowered robe is belted with a long pink sash. His queue falls toward his forehead. Good molding of this bisque nodder, but no marks. Victorian era from Germany. $150.00.

Plate 199. Full figure of elderly gentleman holding a pouch, his bento, the traditional Japanese lunch box, 5". His enlarged head nods and rests on double-hook wires. $95.00 – 110.00.

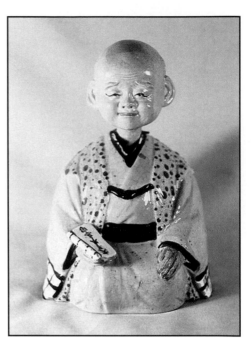

Plates 201 and 202. Two views of a kneeling Japanese elder, 6½". Characters on the book in his right hand translate "Japanese Country." His spotted vest is finished in oatmeal crackle glaze and worn over the kimono tied with a black Judo belt. The braided queue is worn to the crown of his head (a Japanese custom). Condition is very good. The base is solid and the head nods from a bell-shaped counterweight. An unmarked terra-cotta nodder. $175.00+.

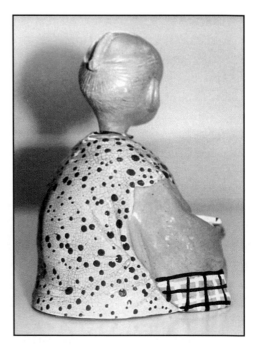

Plate 200. An erect and distinguished white-haired elder sits on a woven mat in typical Japanese fashion, 7½". He is highly glazed terra cotta, except for his head and hands. While he pours sake into a cup, he nods agreeably from the long metal counterweight inside his body. An unidentified oval mark with Japanese characters is impressed on the solid base. $450.00.

Plate 205. Two kneeling Japanese ladies wearing same kimono but with different heads, 6". Terracotta clay. A colorful striped robe is worn over the kimono that is wrapped with the traditional obi. The spice jar they hold was molded separately, placed in their hands, painted, and fired. Solid base. Inverted bell-shaped lead counterweight. Good condition. $235.00 each.

Plate 203. Japanese man seated on a stump, 5". His eyes are squinted, he yawns and reveals a toothless mouth. The gourd in his hand has been carved into a container. His black queue curls at the crown of his head, and he is an excellent nodder. $100.00.

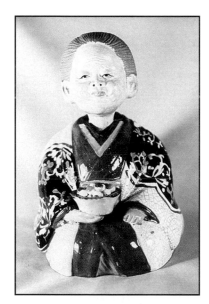

Plate 206. Kneeling elderly with wrinkled face, pleasant countenance, and gray hair, 6¼". Terracotta clay. Her crackle-glaze robe is embroidered with a floral design. She holds a bowl of colorful bird eggs, separately molded and placed in her right hand. $175.00.

Plate 204. A serene lady plucking her samisen, 3¼". Her highly glazed coat is enhanced with brown trim and baggy pants. Terra-cotta clay. $150.00.

Plates 209 and 210. With feet apart, a young scholar holds an open book, 6¼". The belted apron over full ankle-length pants almost conceals sandaled feet. Her black hair is arranged in an intricate butterfly knot entwined with a red ribbon. The lead counterweight inside her body produces a lively nod. $120.00 – 140.00 as is.

Plates 207 and 208. Barefoot, pigeon-toed peasant holding a basket with a turnip, 8½". She stands on bare clay earth beside a larger basket. $100.00+.

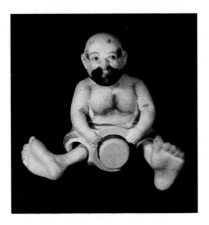

Plate 214. Comical man smoking a cigarette, 3¾". "SHOFU CHINA" in a wreath and mold number 6423. Head swings on wire positioned just above his ears. Movable legs can be pushed into his body cavity and expose only big bare feet. Bare upper torso and green pants. $175.00+.

Plate 211. Kneeling woman is wearing an embroidered kimono wrapped with an obi, 4¾". Her hair is pulled to a tight knot. Hands and face are unglazed terra cotta. Solid base. Lead counterweight. $125.00.

Plate 212. Peasant woman with open book on her lap, 2⅝". She is kneeling on a jar lid and from her used condition she opened many jars. But the jar is missing. Terra cotta with lead counterweight. $75.00 – 100.00.

Plate 213. Mother with small child playing at her feet, 3½". Worn condition. The base is solid, and the small zinc counterweight is attached in the neck via a wire. Excellent nodding action. Terra-cotta composition from late nineteenth century. $90.00 – 125.00 as is.

Plate 215. This miniature nodder is inscribed "JAPAN" on his back, 2¾". He holds a gourd in one hand and clutches a brown cloth sack slung over his shoulder. Terra-cotta clay, worn condition, metal counterweight, and fine wire pierced through his neck. After 1921. $100.00 as is.

Plates 216 and 217. Amusing gossipers, 6¼". Bodies are porcelain with bisque head and hands. Mark: Mold numbers: 6636 A and 6636 B. They are jovial conversationalists with lively wagging tongues and waving hands. Garments are richly embroidered in the chinoiserie style. Action of movable parts is well balanced. Pins and posts are comparable to Plate 244. Excellent condition. After 1934. $450.00 pair.

JAPANESE THEATER

It has been said there is no more polite nation in the world than Japan, and this inherent characteristic is manifest at the theater. A fortunate acquisition of several nodders reflect their traditions. As evidenced in some nodders, general street attire of Japanese men and women tends toward muted colors. Vivid colors were more germane in the theater than on the street.

Recognizable to western civilization is the classic drama of the Nº(h) Theater. A small monkey was trained to "act like a monkey" and delighted audiences before and between performances. He is reported to have originated from a tiny island off the tip of Kyushu. His duty was to dance, amuse, and entertain, using tools of his trade which are waving his fan and ringing his cluster of bells.

The Kabuki theater espouses a bright, popular theme of performing arts. In syllables, Ka–bu–ki translates "Ka" for song, "bu" dance, and "ki" skill. Since the seventeenth century tradition mandated that male actors play all roles. Training began as young as five, and players trace ancestry through generations. Long drawn-out drama continued throughout the day with interludes of farce. The audience watched, ate, slept, or freely came and went. Actors and dancers perform in elaborate and often weighted costumes. Traditionally they portray two or more roles and wear a mask to play multiple parts. Because a masked face is expressionless, the stylized dialogue, dramatic movement, and clever costume changes in full view of the audience will not disturb rhythm of the play. With dancing, music, elaborate sets, and imagination a story is told as the drama unfolds.

Plate 218. A small monkey, 4¾". The solid body of this nodder is baked clay, and his long robe is enameled and baked again. The wobbly head rocks and rests on his neck and he sticks out his loose saucy tongue. His face is unglazed but his headdress appears to be a wrapped extension of his skull. $500.00 rare. The miniature monkey, 2½" is a netsuke. $50.00 not rare.

Plates 219 and 220. These nodding Kabuki actors wear thick liquid powder make-up and face cream applied on a clown-white face, 4". Semi-transparent bisque. Unmarked. $275.00 – 325.00 pair.

He is playing the part of a Geisha. His hair dressing (a wig) is done in classic peach hair, or ginko style. His brilliant yellow kimono is embroidered with bats and chrysanthemums. He plays the samisen (three-stringed musical instrument). Skilled actors were so polished that Japanese ladies attended theater just to watch the "oyama," or "onnagata" and learn gracious ways.

Plates 221 and 222. This actor, with mask pushed on top of his head, is dressed in a cool shade of blue, exemplifying a wicked fiendish character. $275.00 – 325.00 per pair.

BANKO WARE, late Eighteenth Century

Banko is a favorite among collectors and dates from the seventeenth century. The first Banko, Numanami Gozaemon, was a wealthy merchant and amateur potter who lived in the province of Ise. His work and formulas did not die with him, but were rediscovered and continued through a succession of potters. Banko wares regained popularity when displayed at the Paris Exhibition in 1878 and became highly collectible with escalating prices.

Molding was in natural clays with enamel decorations in the late Ming style, also called Swatow ware after the seaport in southeastern Kuangtung. Banko's seal and familiar type of products have been widely imitated. A variety of objects were made, such as bowls, jugs, plates, teapots, vases, and tea sets.

Characteristics of Banko nodders distinguish them from other Orientalia. Banko-faience is delightful and reveals personality of the Japanese peoples. These nodders portray polite, serene composure, other times a pleasing countenance and obvious twinkle in the eye.

Plates 225 and 226. The monkey friend of Sun Wu Kong sits beside a reed basket and holds a carved coconut monkey mask on his knee, 3½". His crackle-glaze plaid vest is tied in front. Counterweight is zinc. Circa late 1800s. $450.00 – 500.00.

Plates 223 and 224. In Chinese legend Sun Wu Kong is the monkey king, 4". His speckled jacket is glazed, and the peach he holds is symbolic of immortality. He bears his teeth, but is revered for mischievous personality traits. Zinc counterweight. $450.00 – 500.00.

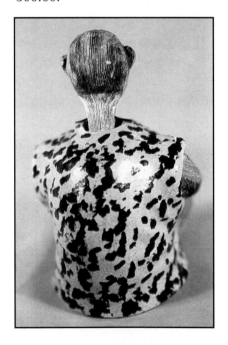

Plate 227. Not only does this happy fellow nod yes, the pet monkey on his shoulder nods with him, 5". That is a drum on his knee and a drumstick in his other hand. $175.00.

Plate 228. Shou Lao, the Chinese Taoist god of longevity, is one of seven gods symbolizing good health and long life, 5½". Seated on the floor, he is portrayed as an elder. Protuberance of his bald head signifies age and wisdom. He nods and waves a hand. Excellent condition. $250.00+.

I purchased Shou Lao with five other nodders at an auction in 1988. An octogenarian couple were moving to town from their large home and disposing of many year's accumulation. They were owned by the affable wife who related how she had acquired six nodders. Soon after their wedding she was surprised when her young husband presented her with a 12-piece place setting of Haviland china. However, she considered the china too delicate and was not pleased. Sometime later she visited a friend's antique shop and became fascinated with six nodders. As a newlywed with no money for extras, she negotiated a trade with her dealer friend...six nodders in exchange for all her Haviland china! I raised my eyebrows and had to ask her husband's reaction. "He was not happy then," she said, "but in time he forgave 'the deed.'" The ensuing fifty years she enjoyed her nodders, always careful to place them beyond reach of growing children and grandchildren. Although she expressed no regrets, many years were to

pass before she acknowledged a foolish trade. Her husband was unable to conceal a sly grin. Now it is my pleasure to appreciate the fine condition and tender care of her cherished nodders.

Plates 229 and 230. This courtly lady stands 10" tall, colorful and highly glazed except for hands and facial features. A white stocking with divided big-toe is visible under her kimono. Excellent post nodder. $125.00 – 175.00.

Plate 231 and 232. The lovely geisha's hands are folded in front of her, 3½". Her larger counterpart, 5", is holding a narcissus. $140.00 large. $125.00 small.

Plate 233. Kneeling lady wearing green headband, 3¾". Holding a fan in her right hand, the entire terra-cotta nodder is glazed, rather unusual because hands and face are usually without glaze. $125.00.

Plate 234. Japanese scholar with nodding head and waving hand, 5". The enlarged forehead of a learned man is a storehouse of knowledge. This entire nodder has been painted and fired, and his open mouth shows teeth. Bell-shaped zinc counterweight cannot be removed from the solid base. Late nineteenth century. $250.00+.

BANKO CHILDREN

Traditionally, small Japanese children are spoiled by the family. Custom mandates an aura of bliss for the young until they reach school age. These happy nodders wear robes with broad shoulder treatment, traditional style of mid-nineteenth century dress.

Plate 235. An exceptional nodder with a mischievous rider astride the back of a curious monkey. The lad nods and kicks his legs to urge the monkey on. 5" x 6". $600.00 rare.

Plate 236. Tableau of mischievous Japanese lads with sparkling eyes and nodding heads, 4". Queues are turned up on partially shaved heads. Faces are smiling and dimpled. Their robes are colorfully glazed. Lad on left also waves his hand, the others hold chopsticks or fans. Interesting counterweights are pear shaped and cannot be removed because they are molded into one piece with the head. Open base and near mint condition. $150.00 – 200.00 each.

Plate 237. Sober faced child with doll-like features, wearing a periwinkle robe, 2½". Straight black hair tied with a big hair bow. Solid base. Metal ball counterweight. Her head can be turned any direction since there are no grooves for a pin to rest in the aperture. $75.00.

Plate 238. Detail on this little Banko child is quite good, 4". A scarf covers just the top of her head. Her sparkling black eyes and pleasant smile seem to nod a teasing no as she sits with legs under her in typical Japanese fashion. $100.00 – 150.00.

Plate 239. Seated smiling child with fan and head covering, 4½". Nods no. $100.00 – 150.00.

After the first world war shoddy imports from Japan were of inferior quality, but after WWII work of Japanese artisans improved to meet the more demanding American market. Import-export business was essential for restructuring Japan and products became plentiful and quite affordable. During the seven year period of American occupation exports were marked "Occupied Japan" or "Made in Occupied Japan."

Plate 240. The colorful Ardalt mark is distinct and easily recognized. The "AA" and "ARDALT" are in bold print, with "Japan," "Lenwile China," and "Hand Painted" included on the crest. Identical numbers, followed by "A" and "B" indicate original pairs that have not been separated. Porcelain figurines may be glazed or bisque, and quality is generally very good to excellent. They are amusing, colorful, and very collectible.

Many were souvenirs of returning servicemen. Threaded pins with holding screws are a distinguishing feature of Ardalts. Unfortunately some of these original pins and screws are missing or have been replaced with a plain wire.

Plate 242. The age of innocence. Mark: ARDALT on each nodder with mold numbers 6529, 6530 A and 6530 B.

These amusing children are good nodders and an amusing spectacle. The young lad in the center is not turning a somersault, 5". He is bending over in a spying position, but if standing erect he would be nine inches tall. His dark kinky head swings on a C-curve post held in place by a threaded neck-pin with holding screws. He is wearing ruffled polka dot shorts with socks rolled down to his ankles. His wide-eyed expression is one of intense interest. $295.00 – 325.00.

The naive black girl's eyes are raised in a look of total innocence and she nods yes, 6¼". Three ribbon bows are tied in tight curls. She discreetly holds polka dot ruffled panties in front of her body, naked except for green socks falling over her big shoes. $350.00 – 400.00.

The chubby child on the left is well dressed from the derby hat perched on kinky curls to white spats covering his shoes, 6½" His amusing expression is the broad grin and gloved hands raised in awe. He encountered the scene by accident. His round tummy is covered with a fancy shirt and colorful bow tie. Pants hang low on his belly. His astonished look makes him nod yes. $225.00 – 350.00.

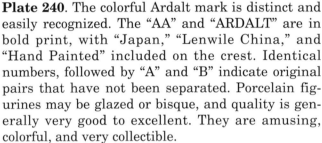

Plate 241. Occasionally different heads are seen on the same body, 5½". Mold number 6532 is identical for both. Legs can be positioned any angle or pushed inside the cavernous body. One is a comical clown and the other becomes a playful child.

Plates 243 and 244. The piano duet, 8½ x 7¼". Bisque. Mark: "Ardalt." Mold numbers: 6635 A and 6635 B. $550.00 – 650.00 per pair.

These sophisticated musicians wear fine embroidered clothes embellished with rich gold trim. Beautiful heads nod on a long weighted post. Hands wave over the piano keys. Lips are parted as if singing. Musical score rests on the keyboards. Arm posts are weighted for movement and curve into the body contour. Post ends are covered with thin rice paper and printed, "registration applied," plus the registered numbers. Piano skirts are richly embossed with clouds and dragons chasing flaming pearls. In the late Liberace's Las Vegas home, visitors enjoyed a group of these nodders on his baby grand piano sitting beside the candelabra.

Plate 245. A royal couple marked with the Ardalt crest, numbered 6634 A and B, 7¼". Their upper torso bends back and forth at the waistline. They relax beside a planter decorated with flowers, vines, and gold embossing. Figurines such as these are of Meissen influence. $275.00 – 350.00 pair.

Plate 246. Nodding couple, seated, legs crossed, waving a fan and hand, 5¼". Mark: Ardalt shield on the lady and mold number 6491 B. Although this couple was purchased at the same time, the gentleman has neither mark nor mold number. This is an example of European influence by Japanese artisans. Although marked Ardalt, quality of this pair is inferior. $200.00 – 225.00 pair.

Plates 247 and 248. An interesting couple molded in thin ceramic and finished in antique gold. The juggler, 9½", nods no and balances balls on the palm of his hands. Mold No 6470. The lady, 7½", nods yes and her right hand plucks the strings of her instrument. Mold No 6835. Although the lady has an Ardalt mark, the man is unmarked but, Ardalt also. $175.00 – 200.00 each.

Plate 249. Bisque juggler and drummer, 6¾" x 7". Rhythmically the lady beats a drum while her companion juggles balls in each hand. Elaborate costumes are highlighted with gilt. No nodders. Mark: Ardalt. Mold number 6492 A and B. Elaborate costumes are highlighted with gilt. $550.00 – 600.00 pair.

Increasing demand and dwindling supply escalates the cost of our collectibles whether they are new or old.

Plate 250. A popular fellow who puts in frequent appearances at garage sales, shops, and on the auction block. He is bisque and a nice nodder. Imported from Japan, Hong Kong, and Taiwan, he has been marketed through shops and various markets. (One dealer said he paid $4 and was happy to sell for $6.) Today this nodder is worth considerably more, prices now range from $35 to $125. WOW! His yes nod is usually very good, and as a new kid on the block he is doing alright for himself! $60.00 – 95.00.

Artists painted children sitting for a portrait, but the potter molded little people in everyday lifestyle. Nodding figurines of the young are amusing and natural as only children can be and creative Victorians adeptly accentuated playful activities and problems of youth.

From 1850 until WWI there was a variety of imports that ranged from papier-mâché to fine porcelain. Most of the figurines in this chapter nod yes.

Plate 251. Tiny blonde twin babies molded together are bundled securely in a fancy blanket. 3⅓" x 2½". Each child has an outstretched arm and their nodding heads are covered with a cap. Translucent bisque from Germany. Late 1800. $500.00.

Plates 252 and 253. Affluent Victorians hired a governess to care for their growing family. However, from the amused expression on her face, discipline may be in doubt with a threatening slipper in one hand and the other arm akimbo. The big sturdy feet support her swaying body as her head nods provocatively. Unglazed porcelain, no marks. Germany. Unusual. $195.00.

Plate 254. A sober little blonde child and her pet kitten are posed in a big chair as for their portrait, 6¾". Color coordinated in pale aqua tones, the nodder is of heavy porcelain. Mold No. 5317. Impressed elbogen mark of Conta & Boehme, Pössneck, Thuringia. 1878 – 1937. $225.00 – 250.00.

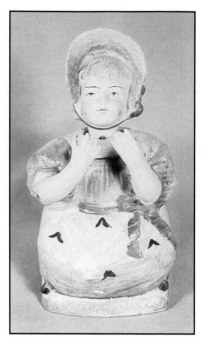

Plate 255. This frolicsome child has anchored herself in a playful position, 7". Legs are straddled as she hugs the candleholder tree trunk. She is dressed in pastels with a matching ribbon in her blonde hair. There is a touch of chinoiserie design on her vest. She nods via a neck pin resting on wires through her body (visible at her shoulders). Glazed porcelain from a German manufactory, late 1800s. No marks. $250.00.

Plate 256. Another lovely blonde child sits on a cushion with legs crossed under her skirt, 5¾". The position of her gesticulating arms and hands molded away from her body is unusual to have survived without damage more than a century. Translucent unglazed porcelain color coordinated in mint green. This child is a no nodder with bell-shaped counterweight. Artist brush number 112, no other mark. This doll-like nodder with mobcap tied under her chin is from the turn of the century when many hatted doll heads were imported to the States from Germany. $250.00.

Condition is quite good with exception of an invisible flaw. Occasionally nodders will have a hidden crack or break in the neck, undetected until the head is lifted such as this nodder. Whether this occurred as the pin was inserted or later is subjective, but damage such as this is not unusual.

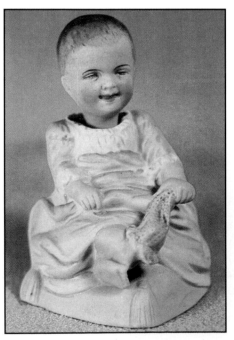

Plate 257. This Heubach-type baby has a talent for teasing, 4". Although wearing a pink nightgown, he is a boy, seated on a pillow with one leg curled under while tugging on his blue sock. Victorians dressed little boys in pink contrary to today's custom, and little girls wore more blue. Translucent unglazed porcelain from Germany. Unmarked. $180.00+.

Some bisque nodders resemble popular piano babies from this era. There is no evidence, but there is similarity to the work of Gebruder Heubach of Lichte, Germany, who molded many moderate priced novelties that were within the price range of middle-class Americans. Heubach, as well as Conta & Boehme and Ernst Bohne Söhne produced many figurines. Eventually the Heubach factory was purchased by Ernst Bohne in 1919.

Plate 259. This comely child sits between two match holders, 5". Basically white with cobalt trim and highlighted with gilt. Bisque from Germany. No marks and the counterweight is not removable. Rare. $125.00 – 200.00.

Plate 258. Small child wearing a pink dress grasps the woven match-striker basket with both hands, 4". Her blue eyes match the hair ribbon. Translucent porcelain unglazed. Heubach type. $125.00 – 150.00.

Plates 260, 261, and 262. Nauseous Chinese twins sit on chamber pots wearing nighties and a scarf tied around their scratchy throats, 4½". To the Germans, little children on pottys were commonly amusing. One lad with flushed face is weaving and straining, but the ashen pallor of his twin brother indicates an upset tummy while his head nods over the woven receptacle. Tossing and turning in bed twisted those black pigtails. The lead cylinder counterweight is less common. Translucent porcelain unglazed. No marks, but excellent condition. Germany. $500.00 pair.

Plate 263. Billy can, Billy can't. Two lads on their pottys, self explanatory. These nodding kids sat on a drugstore counter with cathartic remedies nearby. Chalkware. No price available.

Plate 265. Tough kid with an attitude problem, 6¼". Pudgy fists and threatening eyes are ready to fight. He is braced against an open receptacle, a match holder. Translucent unglazed porcelain, near mint condition. Mold No. 5935. Germany. Late nineteenth century. $275.00.

Plate 264. Chubby child with clasped hands, standing in front of a match holder. Heubach type. $125.00.

Plate 266. This delicate child sits sidesaddle on a silly piglet that lifts one front trotter and nods its head, 2½". Translucent unglazed porcelain. Mold No 564. Near mint. Germany. $200.00+.

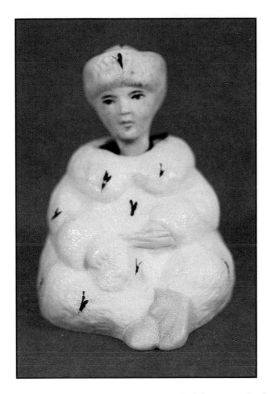

Plate 269. Thousands of Munich Maid beer steins have been manufactured in the vicinity of Munich and sold, not only to local citizens, but to tourists world wide. A foaming stein of beer and bunch of radishes exudes "Gemutlichkeit," good cheer. ¼ L. $100.00.

Plate 267. Miniature Russian child snuggled in a warm fur coat and hat, 2¼". Translucent unglazed porcelain. The pencil-shaped counterweight is one piece molded with the head. Unmarked. Ernst Bohne Söhne, Rudolstadt. $125.00.

Plate 268. Porcelain Muenchener Kindl (Munich Child), 7¼". This pleasing blonde kindl is an official good will ambassador of Munich, the capital of Bavaria. After Germany's victory in the 1870 – 1871 Franco-Prussian War, a new movement evolved and craftsmen were determined their culture would attain renown. Eventually the figure of a monk emerged as the youthful allegorical Munich Maid, still wearing the cowl and robe. This dimpled nodder personifies a fun-loving, mischievous character with comely life-like features. No price available.

The Munich Child is a two-way swayer. One wire is thrust through her temples, another pierces her shoulders. Her left arm cradles a big radish and the missal (book) she holds is embellished with a gold cross. In her other hand is a stoneware stein of foaming beer. No marks.

Plate 270. Altar boy, 9". His duty is to swing the thurible (censer) by its chain. A two-way swayer of highly glazed terra-cotta pottery. Hot coals placed in the lower portion of the censer with incense sprinkled on top emitted a white aromatic smoke. Swung back and forth during Mass and other special ceremonies in the Catholic Church symbolized prayers of the faithful ascending to God. Excellent condition. "Made in Portugal" impressed in the base. Dated 1903 and signed. $300.00.

Plate 272. Gray donkey head hanger with three gleeful youngsters up, 8½". Delicate pastels but no nodding action by the children. $300.00 – 400.00.

Plate 271. Victorian lad sitting sidesaddle on his donkey, 7¾" x 6½". Dressed in a fancy suit and jockey cap atop his blond curls, he does not nod. Rather, the gray donkey is a head hanger and the wire piercing the donkey's neck is visible on the red halter. Excellent unglazed porcelain from Germany. No marks. $375.00.

Plate 273. Another unglazed bisque donkey head hanger, 6½" x 5½". Two billikin kids are riding, but the last one is holding on. $300.00 – 400.00.

Plate 274. Lovely blonde teen-age girl with roses adorning her bonnet, 8". She holds another garland in her hands as her body and head sway. Fine glazed porcelain in excellent condition. Early 1900, Germany. $300.00+.

Plate 276. The charming Dutch child is from Germany, late nineteenth century. She spreads her apron with a graceful side to side sway. Fine glazed porcelain in excellent condition. $200.00 – 225.00.

Plate 277. Miniature ceramic Dutch children, 3". Their water pails, suspended from shoulder yokes, produce sounds of a tinkling bell as they bounce and sway from a strong coil spring. "Hand Painted Delft Blue" © D.A.I.C. New today, but worthy of adding to any collection. $16.00.

Plate 275. A young girl with long black curly hair, 5¼". Her bouffant flowered skirt sways gracefully. Fine glazed porcelain in excellent condition. Early 1900, Germany. $150.00 – 225.00.

Plate 278. Tough kid in a derby hat smoking a big cigar and standing on an ashtray. A flexible steel strap connects his body and head to produce a strong nod. Fine detail but worn paint. This nodder has also been painted as a black kid. Early 1900. "Made in Austria." Very good reproductions have come from Japan. $150.00+ as is.

Plate 281. And dad said, "Be a Man!," 4". He needs more than a black derby hat and big cigar to appease dad. Impressed Schäfer & Vater mark and mold No.8637. $375.00+.

SCHÄFER & VATER WHIMSIES

The Schäfer & Vater mark is discussed in Something Else.

Plates 279 and 280. "Made out of Fathers old ones," 4¾". This uncomfortable kid hides behind a big leaf. Then there is the behind view that bares all. The Schäfer & Vater mark is faint. $350.00+.

Impressed Schäfer & Vater mark. No color.

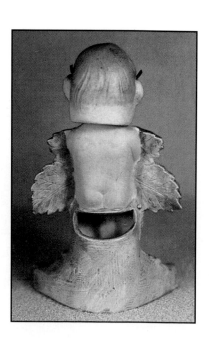

Plate 282. This impish kid's head sways on his condensed body with fingers and soles of his feet resting on a pin-tray base, 7½". Excellent condition except for a replaced wire through his head. Most nodding Schäfer & Vater's are unglazed, this one of glazed porcelain is less common. Impressed mark is distinct. Mold No. 7192. $250.00+.

AFRICAN-AMERICAN CHILDREN

Plate 283. A limited edition of these adorable miniature twins were handmade by artist/sculptor Sandy Srp of Seven Hills, Ohio, 2½". Adding to their charm, they are salt and pepper shakers. With slight encouragement their jovial little heads shake vigorously. The little fellow in a yellow shirt is for salt, his twin is pepper. They are as irresistible as their table use is impractical because they would hold only a few grains of condiment. Glazed porcelain. Mint condition. Circa 1993. $50.00.

Plate 284. The lad's spotless white suit is a stark contrast to his very dark skin, but he obviously enjoys a huge slice from the big watermelon he straddles, 4½". Although shoeless, he is proud of the jockey cap on his head. This excellent nodder came into the States from South America and appears to be of German origin from the turn of the century. Unglazed porcelain. $325.00 – 400.00.

Plate 285. A small brown baby is in the all together and riding on the back of a turtle, 2¾" x 3½". Head and tail of turtle swing on suspended wires. Painted and fired bisque. $75.00 – 85.00.

Plate 286. Black school children, 5" – 5¼". Painted and fired bisque. The boy is proud of his slate and shares knowledge with his friend. Zinc cylinder weights balance the nodding heads. Circa 1890s. Made in Germany. $400.00 pair.

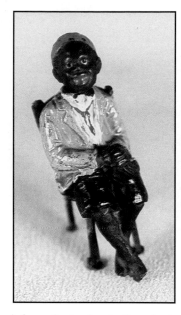

Plate 287. A barefoot plantation lad sitting on a metal chair nods vigorously from the flexible steel strap inside his body, 3¾". Although his condition is somewhat worn, he is well dressed in coat and tie and red skull cap. The entire zinc mold is painted in colorful enamel. $225.00 as is.

Some bobbin' head black children are molded in clay pottery, others are papier-mâché, composition, or plastic. They are found at auctions, shows, flea markets, and garage sales. Sometimes they hold colorful fruit and wear a straw hat if it has not been lost or discarded. An open slot for a money box is common. Sizes range from 3¾" to 7". Usual marks are "Japan," "Made in Taiwan," or more recently "Product of China." They were mass produced after WWII and marketed as souvenirs from areas such as Puerto Rico and Florida.

Plate 288. $45.00.

Plate 289. $85.00.

Plate 290. $45.00.

KISSING KIDS

A variety of "Let's Kiss" children are another appealing souvenir since WWII. Their cute little heads bob up and down on a neck spring while magnetic lips sustain their kiss. Composition is papier-mâché and some were intended as money boxes. Sometimes marked "FOREIGN" or "Japan."

Plate 293. $40.00 – 60.00.

Plate 291. $40.00 – 60.00.

Plate 294. $40.00 – 60.00.

Plate 292. $35.00 – 50.00.

Plate 295. The little Indian chief rocks and bobs but has lost his kissing playmate. $30.00.

Love of pets and their response to human affection is therapeutic without regard to gender. Nodding animals are fascinating whether they are life-like, fictional, or capricious.

Fine porcelain animals are less common, but there is a great selection from pottery, ceramic, metal, celluloid, plastic, composition, wood, and papier-mâché. Animals are covered in genuine hide, real fur, realistic flocking, and fabric. Aside from a nod, there are head hangers, twirlers, and springers. Whatever your preference, old or new(er), they are collectible. Some were intended for shelf decoration. Others came from a child's playroom and later relegated to the archives to reappear at an auction or dealer's showcase. An animated menagerie is out there.

Animals are pictured elsewhere in other chapters.

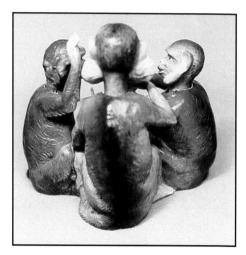

Plates 296 and 297. A porcelain trio of comical primates sitting around a pedestal table for a game of cards, 5" x 5¾". The center dominant monkey has a nodding head and wagging tongue. His two companions also nod. Their deck of playing cards is marked with spots and numbers. Fine color and detail. This rare nodder is an excellent example of the potter's talent to portray three monkeys in three different poses, expressions, and gestures in one animated statuette. Germany. Late nineteenth century. $565.00 – 600.00.

Plate 298 and 299. The gray monkey, with bushy-haired cheeks nods his head and wags his tongue, 5". $300.00 – 350.00.

The smaller brown monkey nods yes and holds a feather fan. All counterweights are metal except for the small monkey with a pear-shaped weight of bisque. No marks. Germany. Late nineteenth century. $100.00 – 150.00.

Plate 300. Molded and fired clay, 2½". This quirky monkey can sit or be suspended from a visible wire loop on his humped back. Its lively head and tail movement "acts just like a monkey." The sculpted body has great detail. $75.00 – 90.00.

Plate 303. A pair of well-marked turtles sitting on a log that is 2½" long. Head and appendages of these miniatures are so perfectly balanced that the slightest vibration activates lively motion. Fine wood carving of unknown origin. $15.00.

Plate 301. Dasypus novemcinctus is the armadillo, 4¾" x 1¼". Armadillos have spread from Mexico as unwelcome intruders into many southern states. They can be infected with leprosy and are used for experimentation. The turtle is a miniature, 2" x 2½". Both are fired clay. Their protective bony plates conceal wires to the head and tail for realistic movement. Impressed "MEXICO." Armadillo, $45.00. Turtle, $15.00.

Plate 304. Gold and silver lively turtles in a glass covered box. Product of China purchased in San Francisco Chinatown. Circa 1994. $28.00.

Plate 302. A ceramic head hanger souvenir of Mexico, 2¾ x 4¼". Glazed and fired with bold design. $25.00.

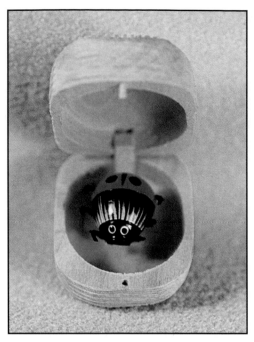

Plate 305. Another little wiggly insect. New, from China. $2.00.

Plate 306. Pink plastic pig head hanger, 2" x 4". Embossed Germany. $75.00.

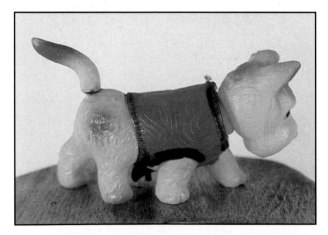

Plate 307. Plastic Scottish terrier head hanger wearing a red coat, 3" x 4¾". Made in Occupied Japan. $75.00.

Plate 308. Porcelain razorback hog with excellent detail and marking, 2½" x 4½". The original wire pin visible at the withers anchors nodding movement of this head hanger. No marks but of German origin, possibly late 1800s. $200.00.

Plate 309. Nodding pug dog and frozen spaniel, 4⅝". Painted and fired porcelain. No mark. Spaniels with long silky hair were the favorite breed of Charles II. Englishmen loved the pug with a profile resembling a clenched fist. Breeding pugs gained popularity in the seventeenth and eighteenth centuries. They are believed to have come through Japan, from China, and into Europe. $100.00 – 150.00.

Plate 310. Pleasing bisque pets, good modeling and marking, sitting erect on hind quarters, 5¼". Left to right, a siamese cat, a bulldog with hollow eye sockets wearing a hat, and spaniel dog. Amber glass eyes of the spaniel are original; green eyes of cat were affixed by former owner. Post nodders. No marks. $175.00 each.

Plate 311. Cockatoo, 6⅝". Painted porcelain of excellent translucent quality. A heavy lead weight inside the body activates a nodding head as the bird sticks out its tongue from inside wires. This life-like bird has a yellow and pink crest, white plumage, and piercing glass eyes. Black claw feet grip the tree branch. Mint condition. Germany, late nineteenth century. Rare. $300.00 – 375.00.

Plates 312 and 313. The owl is a symbol of wisdom with a book under one wing, 6¾". Being a nocturnal bird, potters had an affinity for owls because both stayed awake throughout the night. The owl was company for the potter whose nocturnal vigil was to tend his oven. Fine porcelain of semi-translucent quality. Amber rhinestone eyes were affixed by a former owner who considered the hollow indentation "ghostly." Germany, late nineteenth century. $250.00 – 300.00.

Plate 314. A pair of glazed iridescent porcelain ducks with nodding heads. The duck on the right is stamped "GERMANY." The other duck sitting beside a baby-chick emerging from the shell is marked "Made in Japan." It is a great look-alike copy from Japan. Germany, $50.00. Japan, $35.00.

Plate 316. Alligator ashtray, 4" x 4¾". Glazed ceramic. Wings move the menacing upper jaw and a little bird has landed on the open mouth. Japan. Mark: Patent T.T. $95.00.

Plate 315. Boxer head, wagging tongue, alert eyes, and erect ears, 4½". Bisque. Patent 54256. Made in Japan. $115.00.

Plate 317. Porcelain spotted puppy and a mother cow. Heads of these miniatures twirl on their extended pointed necks. Pre-WWII Japan. $45.00 – 75.00 each.

Plate 318. Thelma's curly poodle with yellow bow tie, 5". Head twirls on elongated neck. White glazed pottery from Japan. $30.00.

Plate 321. Painted zinc baby bluebird, 2½". Head nods on flexible strap of spring steel. Early 1900s "GERMANY" in raised letters. Worn condition. $95.00.

Plate 319. Glazed pottery skunk family with fuzzy heads and tails. Colors and molding well done. Mother's head bounces on spring action, but her chained youngsters are frozen. $65.00.

Plate 320. Pipe smoking pewter pug sitting on a horseshoe ashtray with an inset carving of a four leaf clover. 3¼" x 5½". Head nods on flexible steel strap. $135.00.

Plate 322. An alert pewter doe, 3½" x 3½". Head moves on flexible steel strap. Excellent detail in casting the animal. $150.00.

Plate 323. Pewter English pointer poised with one paw up, 9" long. Head moves on flexible steel strap. Used condition, possibly a child's toy. Early 1900s. $175.00.

Plate 326. Dachshund head hangers, 6" x 10½". The larger red puppy with black markings, glass eyes, and flocked plastic body wears a gold dog tag on the metal collar. This pristine nodder was advertised in 1992 as "Watchful Waldi" and available through catalog sales, wearing the "Western Germany" tag. The other puppy with a chain collar is good quality and weight. Pre-WWII of German origin. Large, $60.00. Small, $45.00.

Plate 324. A burro, trumpeting elephant, and bear are copper-plated metal made in Japan. A spring steel strap connects the head and body for movement. $25.00 – 35.00 each.

Plate 327. Rin Tin Tin and her offspring are head hangers, like the dachshunds were often seen in rear windows of the automobile. Mother, $85.00. Puppy, $50.00.

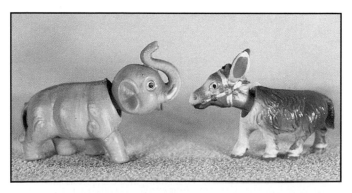

Plate 325. Dealers pair the miniature celluloid donkey and elephant as symbolic of the two political parties. Japan. $25.00 – 35.00 each.

Plate 328. Black and white spotted puppy, 5¾".
Spring neck. Paper label. Japan. $25.00.

Plate 330. Silly donkey with a lively bouncing
head, 5½". Post-WWII. Paper label, Japan. $48.00.

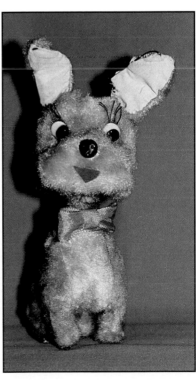

Plate 329. Fuzzy fabric puppy with a spring neck
from Japan, 7". $25.00.

Plate 331. Bushy-tailed donkey head hanger wearing a straw hat and a gold collar, 5¾" x 6". Flocked
plastic. Japan. $30.00.

Plate 332. A surprised young donkey head-hanger with a crop of hair between his ears, chewing on a tulip bulb, 4¾" x 4½". Flocked plastic. Japan. $30.00.

Plate 334. Proud grinning, toothy Mother Fox with glass eyes holds her baby wrapped up like a papoose. Mother Fox is frozen, but when baby is lifted from Mother's paws, the baby nods. Composition. Rare, from Germany. $1,500.00.

Plate 333.

> "I never saw a purple cow,
> I never hope to see one,
> But I can tell you anyhow
> I'd rather see than be one."
>   Attributed to Gelette Burgess

Purple Ferdinand head-hanger wears a gold neck collar, furry topknot, and chews on a plastic orchid, 3¾" x 5½". He is flocked plastic. $35.00.

Plate 335. Chalkware chicken with a strong neck spring. $100.00+.

Plate 336. A strange mythical animal of light weight papier-mâché, 4" x 6". A dog head with mouse ears, tiger body, and cat tail. Head hanger. $100.00+.

Domestic cats are not a rare breed, rather they date back several thousand years to ancient Egypt. However, they were generally neglected by artists who apparently preferred dogs. Ancient Egyptians introduced cats into civilization and for centuries cats were associated with witchcraft. Cats' killer instinct for mice was appreciated, but the superstitious feared them as demons.

A dealer told me a story about the origin of cat house. He said the name originated during the nineteenth century from a cat figure with a paw signed on the underside in script black ink, "E Galle." This pottery cat lived in the window of a French brothel and had a nodding head. Thus, cat house was named. If true, I have been unable to locate a nodding cat with Galle's signature. Emile Galle (1846 – 1904) was a talented French artisan who manufactured a variety of products and much of his work was in pottery. There is need for more research.

Plate 337. Elusive bull moose, characterized in cartoons with a bucket nose and goofy eyes, 4". His most handsome feature is his palmated antlers that spread five feet across from tip to tip. His name means "twig-eater" and the Algonquin translation is "he-strips-bark." Papier-mâché bobbin' head. Paper label, "A mark exclusive." Made in Japan. $38.00.

Plate 338. Orange cat wearing a pearl necklace, 7¾". Concealed spring in neck. Flocked papier-mâché. Paper label Japan. $50.00.

Plate 339. A soft furry kitten, probably a child's toy, 4½". Strong spring in neck. Big black eyes and white ribbon around its neck. $245.00.

Plate 341. Comical cat with green eyes and spring neck, 10". Plastic with flocked gray coat. A money box. Royalty Designs, Inc. © Miami, Fla. N/A

Plate 340. Playful family of black cats, papa, mama, and two kittens, 5¼". Furry top-knots and tails. Concealed neck spring. Pottery. Japan. $55.00.

Plate 342. Green-eyed kitten in a basket, spring neck. Enameled wood souvenir from Henry Flager Museum gift shop. Circa 1993. $4.00.

If you collect nodders it is a nodding figurine.
If you collect dolls it is a nodding doll.
If you collect toys it is a nodding toy.
Whatever it is, it is collectible in the eye of the beholder.

At the turn of the century children were an affectionate and humorous subject of the potter, albeit in fun. Some little people were so realistically portrayed their silent sound effects become audible.

People and playthings are ageless and the pleasures of childhood are rekindled in adults. Dormant dreams return as fantasies. When children's toys were beyond bounds of the parental pocket, imaginative youth improvised their own implements of play.

For centuries artists painted people, families, and children with toys and pets, but our performing nodders were relegated to the hands of the potter.

By late nineteenth century amusing and articulated toys appeared on the market to the delight of the young. The novelty of movement inspired German toy makers and their work comprises the majority of Victorian nodders we see today. The industry thrived, especially in production of popular mechanical toys, but nodders whose movement was encouraged by a gentle prod were less plentiful. They were breakable and not altogether intended as playthings.

Some German doll factories, puppenfabriken, patented models of nodding dolls around the turn of the century. Nods were achieved in various ways. Finger pressure on the doll's body induced a yes or no response enabling a child to converse with the doll. Another factory manufactured a doll head with swiveling and nodding movement. Other dolls were molded in several parts and manipulated by strings affixed within the body. To the doll enthusiast they are indeed collectible. However, they may not satisfy the nodder purist because they are not activated by that gentle touch.

Doll collectors equate nodders and dolls. Theoretically they can be a doll, a toy, and/or a nodding figurine. Painted bisque and glazed porcelain dolls with swaying or nodding action were not practical playmates, rather to be admired on a little girl's dressing table, nightstand, or mantle. Surely not carelessly tossed in a toy box! Accidental happenstance and child's play contributed to much damage and scarcity of survival. Also, balancing nodding action was not only tedious and difficult, but a deterrent to production as well.

Plate 343. "Our Darling" is a cute googlie-eyed blonde with an impish sway, 4½". Impressed mark of Schäfer & Vater Porcelain Factory. 1890 until about 1962. Bisque in excellent condition. $225.00.

Plate 344. Swaying of the beautiful little Dutch girl enhances her playful mood with the toy lamb and donkey in her outstretched arms, 4". Excellent condition except for replaced wire through her mid-section. Schäfer & Vater. $225.00.

Plate 345 and 346. Two little girl swayers in bisque, 4½", holding original straw flowers in their hands. Part of their bouquet is missing. The swayer on the left is 5". Both pedestals are marked on the base with the dark blue anchor mark, Plate 345, of Ernst Bohne Söhne. Rudolstadt, Thuringia. 1878 – 1920. $300.00 each.

Movement of these dolls is activated from a wire at the waistline piercing through extended pedestal legs for swaying action. Facial features, molded hair, and clothing are of excellent detail. In the hand of each little swayer is a tiny hole for feathers, a bouquet, or little basket of flowers. Perhaps these figurines occupied a prominent place in some child's room. No doubt adults were interested also. Copies have been reproduced in Japan and so marked.

Plate 347. Bobbie-Mae, 10". A two-way swayer. All original. Composition. A paper label on the bottom of her feet reads: "Bobbie-Mae, Swing and Sway Doll inspired by Sammy Kaye, Mfg: by Wondercraft Co. N.Y." No date. $275.00.

Bobbie-Mae was awarded a first place purple ribbon (still attached on her back) at the Kerville Doll Show in Kerville, Texas. A pivot construction inside her body produces a side to side swaying motion. Some of these dolls were dressed in pink with white trim, others in pastel blue.

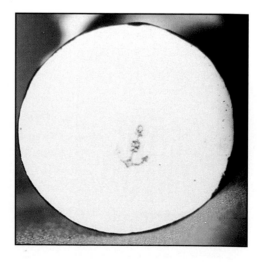

Plate 349. Three look-alike Russian dolls span a half century, 4½". With an arm raised and a hand on the hip, their lively sway simulates a traditional country dance. Dressed in national costume, their head is tied with the elatonk and they wear traditional carashan dress. The beautiful doll with closed eyelids in the center is on loan from a friend and of heavy Bakelite from a 1940 factory in Moscow. Doll on the left is plastic, marked © 1967 L.I.I. Made in Hong Kong. The other doll of lighter quality Bakelite bears the "Made in USSR," mark and Apt.CM -1. $50.00 – 75.00 each.

Plate 348. Denny Dimwit©, 10". Composition two-way swayer. Head and body move in opposite directions. All original. ©1948. This character is from the Winnie Winkle comic strip. $225.00 – 450.00.

Plate 350. The additional set of three Russian dolls, same size and swaying movement, were purchased in September 1995, in the gift shop at the exhibition of The Treasures of the Czars in Topeka, Kansas. A recent import for this exhibition, they are medium weight Bakelite, marked "Made in USSR." They are currently found in shops with other products from Russia. $10.00 each.

Plate 352. When opened six little children dwell within.

Plate 351. Wood nesting dolls, many came from Russia, others from Japan and China. This form of folk art spans many years, unique with painted features, occasionally artist signed. A single wood pin in the neck permits the head to roll. $40.00 pair.

Plate 353. A charming miniature pair are printed O.S.K. Line, and were table favors on a cruise ship. $30.00 per pair.

Plate 354. Later version of painted wooden dolls with nodding heads, 7". $25.00.

Plate 355. Jamaican wooden dolls with hoop earrings, 6½". $25.00.

KNOTTERS

Because the elastic cord connecting head and body is knotted on both ends, they are frequently referred to as nodders, also spelled "knotters." The "nodder" connotation is a misnomer because head movement ceases if the cord is not manipulated for constant encouragement. Thus knotters are not true nodders. The pronunciation is the same, the spelling is different.

As novelties these little knotter dolls were plentiful. In addition to toys, they were party favors and special thoughts for children. Similar bisque knotters were manufactured in Japan, so marked, but of lesser quality.

Plate 356. Miniature pair, delicate and damaged, 2¼". A woman and her clown companion are thin molded celluloid. A spring in the head is weighted to the lead base. Impressed "Germany." Pre-World War II. $35.00 pair as is.

Plate 357. A pair of celluloid children, 3". The lad had been repainted by a previous owner. Heads are attached to the body via an elastic cord, thus the term, knotters. This pair is unusual because they are also rattles. Mark: embossed fleurs-de-lis. Japan. More commonly seen in bisque, but not as rattles. $75.00 each as is.

Plates 358 and 359. This comely young soldier boy is a knotter in excellent condition, 4". Mold No. 11016. Chetney Co, Inc. © Germany. $200.00.

Plate 360. Little blue-eyed girl, colorfully dressed and carrying her pocket purse, 3". Hertwig & Company of Katzhütte. $100.00.

This company was founded in Thuringia, Germany, in 1864, by Christoph Hertwig and partners, Johann Nikolas Beyerman, and son, Benjamin Beyerman. Christoph Hertwig became sole owner in 1869. This company is primarily recognized for production of many fine dolls. During the 1920s, when these knotters were in production the Christoph heirs, Fritz, Ernst, and Hans Hertwig were listed as owners of the company.

Plate 361. Young bisque Indian maiden with feather headdress. Visible hole in left hand. Germany. $150.00.

COMIC KNOTTERS

There is still some kid in all of us. Open the newspaper to the business or sports section but sooner or later we find the funnies and read the latest escapade of our favorite strip.

Among other fascinating collectibles are popular characters from comic strips and folk lore.

After the first World War popularity of these small bisque characters enjoyed a heyday. Radio was coming into the home and television was unknown. Hertwig and Company manufactured them for the American market. In 1929 Marshall Field was given exclusive distribution rights. F.A.O. Schwarz, B. Shackman & Co., and Butler Brothers are also listed as licensed distributors. A favorite cartoon character could be purchased individually or as a set at the five and dime store, inexpensive to collect and interesting to follow. Embossed on the back is the name of the character, and "Germany," and sometimes "Willard." Features and clothing were molded on the body and then painted. Paint may show signs of wear but diminished colors result more from an oven-drying process in use at that time that eliminated a second firing in the kiln. With the most careful cleansing, colors will wash away.

Cost of comic characters was $1.80 per dozen. Market value today of a single comic knotter in prime condition will bring three figures.

Plate 362. Cartoon comic character yodeling and strumming his banjo, 3½". Was the dish in front of him for coin tokens? Bisque painted and fired. Made in Japan. $45.00.

Plate 363. Laurel, the Keystone Cop, and Happy Hooligan, 4". Post nodders of larger size, nodding no. $150.00 – 175.00 each.

Happy Hooligan was probably the first comic knotter to make an appearance. This impulsive but well meaning character was always in trouble with the law and consequently down on his luck, but his readers were sympathetic. Recognized with big eyes and a funny red tin can hat worn at a rakish angle. The strip, written by Fred Opper was started in 1900, copyrighted in 1905, and finally discontinued in 1932 because of the creator's failing eyesight.

Plates 364 and 365. Little Orphan Annie first appeared in 1924 in the *New York Times* written by Harold Gray (1894 – 1968). After seven decades faithful readers follow her plight along with her dog, Sandy, and Daddy Warbucks. Note: Annie's wide open eyes as portrayed in the script, like on the knotter, are an open circle sans pupil. Sandy is frozen. $350.00 set.

Plate 366. The Gumps. Left to right: Tilda the maid, Ching Chow, Chester Gump (Andy's son), Andy Gump, Min (Andy's wife), and the rich Uncle Bim. Missing are the Old Timer and Widow Zander. The facial features of Andy Gump are easily recognized. His character evolved from the plight of a real person whose lower jaw had been surgically removed after suffering from osteomyelitis, a bone infection of the lower jaw. Mark: Germany. $100.00+ each.

The *Chicago Tribune* introduced The Gumps in 1917. Sidney Smith, the creator, died tragically in a car accident just after signing a million dollar contract in 1935. Gus Edison continued the strip but original popularity was never regained.

Plate 367 and 368. Moon Mullins strip. Left to right, Lord Plushbottom, Uncle Willie, Mushmouth, Kayo, and Moon Mullins. Mark "Germany, by Willard." $100.00+ each. Mushmouth, $300.00.

Created in 1923 by Frank Willard for the *Chicago Tribune*, readers of the Moon Mullins strip were fascinated with the lifestyle of this family. Kayo was the little fellow who slept in a dresser drawer but daily watched the world go by sitting atop a bookcase. Missing characters are Emmy, Little Egypt, and Aunt Mamie.

Plate 369. Gasoline Alley. Left to right, Skeezix, Corky, Auntie Blossom (Phyllis), Doc, Rachel, Mr. Wicker, Bill, and Avery. Mark: Germany. $100.00+ each.

The *Chicago Tribune* introduced Frank King's strip in 1919. Baby Skeezix was left on Uncle Walt's doorstep and a sympathetic interest developed for this little guy. Unlike some strips where characters never grow older, Skeezix grew into manhood, married, and had his own family. Over the years, additional characters were introduced.

Plate 370. Winnie Winkle with Perry Winkle, her adopted brother. Not to scale but incised with character's names and BRANNER. Branner started the strip in 1920 and it continued 25 years. Germany. $100.00+ each.

Plates 371 and 372. Smitty, created by Walter Berndt. Introduced through the *Chicago Tribune*–New York Syndicate in 1922, and discontinued in 1973. Left to right are Smitty, Herby, his little brother, and his genial boss, Mr. Bailey. Missing is Spot, Herby's lop-eared mutt. Mark: Germany. $100.00+ each.

TOYS

There is a wonderful assortment of nodding toys from tin, cast-iron, wood, ceramic, papier-mâché, celluloid, and plastic. They are humorous, whimsical, and colorful. Those of sturdy construction, like metal or wood, better withstood childish abuse. A fatter Victorian wallet and mail-order catalog brought more toy makers into the act and convenient buying opportunities for home shoppers. By 1862 F.A.O. Schwarz began in New York City and is still in business. The Schlesinger Company was producing an assortment of tin toys in 1975. Two New York companies, B. Shackman & Company and Butler Brothers were wholesale suppliers for other companies. Butler's advertisements stated, "Our price to one is our price to all" and "Goods well bought will sell themselves." Marshall Field & Co., Butler Brothers (later City Products Corp.), Montgomery Ward & Co., and Sears Roebuck & Co. imported the majority of toys until World War I.

The 1912 Sears Roebuck & Co. catalog listed "finest quality pet voice animals with growling voice, a metal pull ring, bushy neck collar, wheels, good expression." Priced from 95¢ to $2.97. Montgomery Ward & Co.'s 1894 catalog advertised imported miscellaneous shaking-head animals with natural finish, sold in an assortment for 10¢ each, cheaper @ 81¢ per dozen, or in lots of 6 dozen or more @ 78¢. A strong cardboard dog that wiggled and swayed back and forth when pulled could be purchased for 35¢.

In 1912, Sears Roebuck & Co listed a leather covered cow (11" x 9") "with moving head and life-like voice on wheel platform" for 95¢. Woolworths and Kresge Ten Cent Stores sold many of these toys. Mr. F.W. Woolworth made annual buying trips to Europe, taking his wife and three young daughters with him.

German toy makers produced a variety of toys. Victorians appreciated their intrinsic value but toys also were an educational tool to develop creativity, patience, and power of concentration, versus the more commercial thrust of toys today.

Quality of porcelain and bisque ranged from excellent to acceptable. Composition and papier-mâché was used because it was adaptable, practical, and inexpensive to manufacture.

The 1894 the Montgomery Ward & Co. catalog pictured and described a "toy elephant with natural skin on platform with wheels, swinging head and fancy colored blanket," 8" x 3½". Price was 30¢ each. A larger size, same description but mounted on concealed rollers under each foot @ 90¢. The 1908 Butler Bros. catalog had a nodding head elephant at 89¢ per dozen. Surviving collectibles resurface today at toy auctions and antique shops with escalated prices.

Celluloid was inexpensive to produce and a popular medium for toys and dolls. After decades of exposure celluloid becomes fractured, discolored, and brittle. Simple toys were made to be played with and many did not survive.

Toy making was a useful cottage industry in Germany, and Nurenberg remains the hub of toy manufacturers. Excellent toys from Japan were also marketed.

Plate 373. Puck was Shakespeare's mischievous sprite in *Midsummer Night's Dream* and from his appearance he has been misbehaving, 3". Zinc. A flexible steel strap connects the body and head for a vigorous nod. Victorian era. Germany. $145.00 as is.

Plates 374 and 375. Growling Boston terrier pull toy, stands 14" x 18". Maker unknown. Sturdy wood-pulp-glue construction. $650.00.

This toddler's playmate is a toy on wooden wheels. Pulled with the chain, the dog's head sways, the mouth opens, and he growls. Big glass eyes are alert and markings are quite realistic. The lower jaw is overshot, the neck is thick, and strong limbs are out at the elbow with turned out toes. The neck collar is stiff bristles.

Plate 376. Two head hangers, the pig and camel are covered with fine kidskin leather. Papier mâché, glass eyes, legs and hoofs are carved wood. The camel's ears are missing along with neck and tail hair. The pig is from France. Pig, $250.00. Camel, $50.00.

Plate 377. Toys with metal springs produced bouncing movement. A painted wooden Dutch waterboy, 9". He is a sturdy swinger from his neck and arms to the buckets he carries. Additionally he is a child's money box. To retrieve coins, a screw on his left side separates the box at the waistline. Made in Spain. Miniature wood waterboy, 3". Made in Spain. Large, $35.00. Small, $15.00.

One waterboy is missing here. The small boy, missing, carried red buckets.

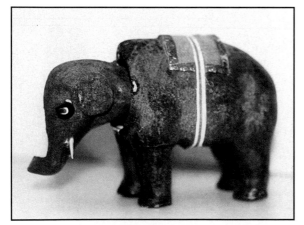

Plate 378. Jumbo, a circus elephant head hanger, 3½" x 5¼". The anchored weight inside his neck produces swinging head motion. Papier-mâché. Early 1900 from Germany. Several sizes were available both larger and smaller, often modeled with a blanket strapped on the animal's back. $65.00.

Late in the nineteenth century, P.T. Barnum, ever the showman and entrepreneur, purchased a live 6½ ton African elephant from the London Zoo for his traveling circus. This gigantic pachyderm was called Jumbo, beloved by children and a star circus attraction. Barnum capitalized on the animal's popularity so it is no surprise toy elephants became a popular child's toy.

Plate 379. A trumpeting gray elephant. Smooth painted papier-mâché head hanger with glass eyes and ivory tusks. Visible evidence inside this elephant are Japanese characters on scraps of newspaper print. Excellent nodder but not excellent condition. Early 1900. $75.00.

Plate 381. The celluloid lamb is mounted on a metal platform with big red wheels. When pulled, the large front wheels raise and lower to give the frolicking lamb a nodding head as well. Excellent condition, from Germany. $95.00.

Plate 380. Camel head hanger saddled with blanket and baskets, 8" x 6½". Glass eyes, papier-mâché body, and wood legs covered with soft fabric. Metal ball counterweight in neck. $175.00.

Plate 382. Roly-poly Keystone Cop, 7½". When he rolls over he shakes his head from the spring inside his rotund body. Papier-mâché. A. Schoenhut Company. Circa 1910 – 1920. $450.00.

The Schoenhut family came to America from Wurtenburg, Germany, and settled in Philadelphia. As skilled woodcarvers their toys were highly regarded and several generations of the family continued the business until it closed in 1935. Their toys were advertised as "costing a little more, but it pays to buy them because they are real quality."

GAMES
By 1892 games were advertised and marketed through Marshall Field & Co.

Plate 383. Game of the Goose. Printed in Bavaria. J.W. Spear & Sons, London. Circa 1915. This board game was sold in 1984 at a toy show in Washington D.C. for $250. Occasionally an individual goose from the set has appeared on the market. $50.00 – 75.00 each goose.

Four people were required to play this amusing board game using the four nodding composition geese. Each goose stands on a different color base and nods provocatively as players take their turn to move their goose. The geese follow a path on a board similar to the Monopoly board game.

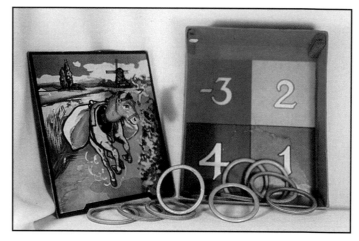

Plates 384 and 385. Whoa–Neddy! A box game for children. Spear's Games, Registered in Great Britain and Canada. Manufactured at Spears Works, Bavaria. Designed in England. Copyright. Brit. Patent Applied for D.R.G.M. (Deutsches Reichs Gebrauchsmuster). Circa early 1900s. $125.00.

"Hee-haw, Hee-haw" says Neddy, nodding, "come and try."

Instructions in the box lid:

"Whoa! Neddy, don't run away" cries the miller as he runs as fast as he is able to catch his wandering animal. Come along and help to throw the colored rings over Neddy's head or ears. He will then have to stop running.

Instructions for playing the game:

"Fix the figure in the slot of the small wooden base. Each player stands the same distance away and tries to throw the rings over Neddy's long ears. If successful, the player scores 5. Should the ring miss and fall on to one of the colored markings on the board, only the number shown on that particular color is scored. Where minus 3 is thrown, this naturally has to be deducted from the total score. Players each throw all the rings one after the other, and the one whose score at the end is highest is the winner." J.W. Spear & Sons.

"GRANDMA WENT TO ENGLAND," a Nodding Game for active children.

A friend told me about this "quiet" parlor game played with young friends in the early 1900s. What a great pastime on rainy days and how times have changed! It could be played by any number of children sitting on chairs in a circle.

Child No.1 began the game with one motion telling what Grandma brought back from England.

The game progressed in this manner.

Child No. 1 turned to child No. 2 on right and said, "Grandma went to England."

Child No. 2 asked, "What did she bring back?"

Child No. 1 answered, "She brought back a "fin-fan" (finger). With this answer, No.1 child began to wave one hand.

Child No. 2, mimicked the fin-fan motion, faced No.3 on right and said, "Grandma went to England."

No. 3 child asked, "What did she bring back?"

No. 2 child responded, "She brought back a fin-fan," and waved one hand. This same question and answer was repeated around the circle until each player waved one hand.

The next round, questions and answers were repeated and action was a another fin-fan (now both hands were waved). This continued as each player in turn mimicked the motion.

After waving two fin-fans, two tap-taps of their feet were added, then a nod-nod of the head, and finally a blink-blink of the eyes.

The game concluded with the entire group mimicking Grandma's action — waving both hands, tapping both feet, nodding heads, and blinking both eyes.

NODDING PENNY TOYS

Entertainment of Victorian children was sometimes limited but generally supervised in contrast to today's youth. The visiting circus, carnivals, county fairs, and itinerant hawking peddlers were excitement of the day. Investment of a penny from the child's pocket required thought. Several pennies were wealth indeed. Toys such as these were barely affordable to the poorest child.

Christmas stockings were stuffed with little treasures like the penny toys, some delicious candy, fruit, and nuts, or whatever Santa could afford. A box of Cracker Jacks was another treasure trove of hidden prizes. Some toys were animated, some were frozen, and a few are found today.

Depression years produced a variety of flimsy penny, nickel, and dime toys at lowest possible cost, many from Japan. Those of tin with movable parts were once plentiful and inexpensive. Today such trifles are scarce, expensive, and very collectible. When available, they are usually found in play-worn condition.

Plate 386. Tin pull toy. Blue goose with a nodding neck stands on a yellow cart with four black wheels. Excellent color and detail. $300.00+.

Plate 387. Nodding tin elephant pulling blue and yellow two-wheeled cart. Unusual and rare. $500.00.

Plate 388. Enameled metal Bambi nods from a wire connecting neck and head, 3¼". Good weight and sturdy. $30.00+.

MODERN NODDING TOYS

Age is no barrier for collectors and the new nodding toys appeal to the young at heart.

Small life-like toys were imported from Germany with a legible paper label of the S.A. Reider & Co., N.Y.C. Copyright. Circa 1920 – 1940. From time to time sturdy little toys of celluloid, Bakelite, and plastic are found with the S.A. Reider label intact.

Celluloid was the first important plastic, an invention of the American chemist, John Wesley Hyatt (1837 – 1920). Hyatt mixed cotton pulp with camphor and other solvents. Working with his brothers they began manufacture in 1872. Celluloid closely resembled ivory, tortoise shell, and horn, and became an affordable commercial substitute for more expensive products such as toilet articles, jewelry, and buttons. Although it was easily damaged and highly flammable it was economical, also light weight and suitable for the toy industry.

Bakelite was sturdy, a synthetic thermosetting resin. It was invented by Belgian-born chemist, Lee Hendrick Baekeland (1863 – 1944), and named for him. Unlike celluloid it was difficult to burn, but emitted harmful fumes under intense heat. By early 1900 it was a successful plastic substitute and popular for costume jewelry. Dubbed the aristocrat of plastics, it was practical for many articles, including nodding toys. True Bakelite is black, dark brown, blue, green, or maroon.

S.A. REIDER & CO. TOYS

These sturdy celluloid and Bakelite nodding toys are found with an S.A. Reider & Co. paper label. Young(er) and old(er) children have (and still do) collect and enjoy them.

Plate 389. Motion of the turtle's head and tail have lively turtle movement. Embossed, "Made in Germany." $25.00.

Plate 392. Quizzical yellow duckling with bouncing head and open beak. Worn paint. S.A. Reider & Co. label. $25.00.

Plate 390. Amusing Dachshund with a nodding head and wagging tail, 5¼". © NYC. Germany. $50.00 – 75.00.

Plate 393. Three celluloid donkeys, excellent nodders, with different celluloid neck pins. These toys were made in Germany. $15.00 – 45.00 each.

Plates 391. A gaggle of geese. One of these little celluloid geese was a plaything of my neighbor's daughter in the 1930s. It has a paper label, "S.A. Reider & Co., N.Y.C Copyright, Made in Germany" and is identical to later look-alikes photographed here together. The goose-neck movement is amusing and quite realistic. $45.00 each.

Plate 394. More S.A. Reider toys from between the two World Wars. $20.00 – 40.00 each.

BREBA © TOYS

This mark has been used since World War II and the variety of nodding toys are appealing and popular. They are usually Bakelite and/or plastic. The mark is embossed BREBA © and W. Germany, or Made in Germany. Since re-unification the recent mark is GERMANY. You will find them in gift shops, stalls, flea markets, and advertised as "Old Fashioned Nodders." Sold abroad also. $15.00 – 20.00 each.

Plate 395.

Plate 397.

Plate 396.

Plate 398.

MORE DIME STORE STOCK

Plate 399. Big horn ewe with suckling lamb. Gray celluloid head hanger. Old dime store stock. No mark. $20.00.

Plate 400. Strutting donkey head hanger. Well molded in lightweight celluloid. Made in Occupied Japan. Large, $75.00 – 100.00. Small, $35.00 – 50.00.

Plate 401. Another 10¢ item before dime stores went out of business. These miniature plastic guys rock on their big feet shaking their heads on a spring neck, 3¾". Printed price on the display box was 29¢ each. "Made in Hong Kong" © BRABO. Imported by Imperial Toy Corporation © 1970 Los Angeles, California 90021. $2.00 each.

Indisputably salt is indispensable and rife with superstition. When you spill it, throw more over your left shoulder. If asked to pass the salt in Kentucky, first set it on the table. Never, never pass from hand to hand "ere bad luck be-fall you."

Although accepted with casual indifference, history relates many interesting tales. Elaborate salt cellars were in use four centuries ago, but England is credited with the production of salt and pepper shakers from the mid-nineteenth century as they are known today.

Containers range from elegant to mundane. Many great sets were manufactured in the USA. Excellent ones came from Germany. The nodding shakers from Germany are quite desirable. But many nodding souvenir sets came from Japan and date prior to WWII.

A predominance of souvenir shakers made an appearance between the two World Wars. Many sets were an advertising gimmick for products. Mom and Pop wayside stations, souvenir shops, and catalogs were likely sources. They were novelties, void of practical use. Now they are eagerly sought by collectors, especially those that nod and what great little collectibles they have become.

An active Salt and Pepper Novelty Shakers Club is international in scope and has more than a thousand members. Regional chapters meet during the year to share fellowship, learn, buy, sell, and/or trade among the members. Once a year they assemble for an annual convention. Every annual convention features a souvenir set of shakers and several times the sets have been nodders.

Nodding shakers are as varied as the materials from which they are made — china, pottery, ceramic, clay, metal, wood, glass, Bakelite, plastic, or chalkware. Figurals are especially pleasing. Most common are sets that nod on a long or squarish hand-painted ceramic or porcelain box. Unique to these nodders is the molded wings in lieu of metal pins, discussed in Construction of Nodders. A gentle touch produces a swinging or nodding action. Salt and pepper is stored in the counterweight that rests in the base. The idea is equally novel and impracticable, containing comparatively few grains of salt and pepper.

The Nippon mark was mandatory from 1891 to 1921. After that Nippon became Japan and was printed in English. Consequently, from 1921 until World War II many nodding sets were marked "Japan," "Made in Japan," and/or "Patent T.T." During the period of American occupation until 1952, all exports from Japan had to be marked "Made in Occupied Japan," or "Occupied Japan." Signing of the peace treaty on April 28, 1952, discontinued the "Occupied" mark. Paper stickers were permitted but many were washed away and lost over the years. Thus some collectibles appear unmarked, though generally recognizable to the collector.

Shoddy Japanese exports from previous years lingered in the American mind, necessitating better quality to meet standards of a more discerning public. Japanese artisans copiously copied and manufactured designs of other well-known manufacturers, and their work was quite good.

Plate 402. Nodding salt and pepper bear cubs stand in a ceramic box. Five Olympic rings are representative of five continents of the original participants. (Note: the fifth ring is yellow, barely visible.) $200.00 – 300.00. Teddy bear, $45.00.

Every Olympic year has an official mascot and in 1980 the Russian bear was symbolic of that country's vast size, culture, and strength. Two miniature bear cubs in this nodding set sit upright in the protective shadow of their big brown teddy bear wearing his Olympic belt. This teddy bear was an emblematic souvenir of the 1980 Olympiad.

Plate 403. The tag on teddy's tail.

FIGURALS...PEOPLE, ANIMALS, AND ANTHROPOMORPHICS

Figural shakers, people and animals, are less common and more costly. Naughties are amusing and popular.

Plate 404. Native Indian boy playing music to charm the cobra from its woven basket. Notice the boy's bulging cheeks as he blows into the pipe. He is the salt, 3¼", the cobra, 4", is pepper. Patent T.T Japan. $200.00+.

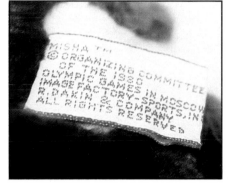

Plate 405. Cowboy nods his head, waves one gun, and holds another, 3½". Made in Japan. Patent T.T. $175.00+.

Plate 406. This Thai couple are bobbin' head shakers with condiment holes on the back, 4¼". Plastic. Paper label, Japan. $50.00.

Plate 408. Babies in diapers. Seated blonde baby, no nodder. Babe on back is frozen. Paper label, "Sarsaparilla Deco Designs" West New York, New Jersey. Circa 1984. Japan. $30.00 – 45.00.

Plate 407. These two nodding Dutch kids are too far apart to kiss. Souvenir from Peterboro, Canada. Patent T.T. Japan. $50.00 – 85.00.

Plate 409. Two young people on an outing to catch butterflies walk arm in arm. He nods no, but she nods yes, 3¾". Patent T.T. from Japan and marked FOREIGN. $150.00+.

Plate 410. The Clintons nod on the White House roof, 4½" x 6". The President nods yes. Mrs. Clinton nods no. Advertised as first set of HEADS OF STATE, "Nodders Collection." © "Made in China" 1994. $25.00.

Plate 412. "Ol' Mac Donald." The pig truck driver is hauling a chicken sitting on a nest of eggs. Clay Art, Made in China. Circa 1995. $25.00.

Plate 411. A reversible Dutch Girl standing on a bell, holding two glass jugs that are salt and pepper shakers, 3½". The metal bell rings from a metal clapper and when shakers touch the bell, there is more sound. Also collected by ABAII members. $10.00 – 15.00.

Plate 413 and 414. A pair of anthropomorphic pigs wearing clothes, strut hand in hand, 3¾". Wings support their heads for a nod. Granule holes are gold snouts. Pottery. "Made in Japan," Patent T.T. $150.00 – 200.00.

Plate 415. A pair of monkeys beat drums on the back of a colorful reclining camel, 3¼" x 4¾". "Made in Japan," Patent T.T. $250.00 – 300.00.

Plate 417. Kangaroo mother with baby joey in her pouch, 4". Mother nods yes. Baby says no. "Made in Japan," Patent T.T. $60.00 – 85.00.

Plate 416. Walking elephant with clown and dog riders, the salt and pepper shakers, 3¼" x 5¼". Red stamp on the bottom of the elephant's foot, "Made in Japan." There are other color variations and designs of this set. $350.00+.

Plate 418. Perky black mama cat and her peppery kitten both nod yes, 3". Patent T.T, "Made in Japan." $200.00+.

Plates 419 and 420. An unusual and amusing set of monkey shakers, 2½". The monkey's head twirls on the spike. Red stamp, Japan. $100.00 – 125.00.

Plate 421. A gray mama monkey nods yes, but her baby says no, 3¼". Patent T.T, Japan. $75.00.

Plate 422. Anthropomorphic mother cow embraces twin babies with pacifiers between their lips. The calves are the nodders. Blue underglaze CLAY ART, Handpainted, ©1994, Made in China. $22.00.

Plate 423. This donkey is a head hanger. As a beast of burden, the milk cans on his back are for salt and pepper, 4¼" x 6¼". Paper label Vcagco Ceramics. Japan. $75.00.

Plate 425. "What's Cookin." Anthropomorphic stove with soup kettle and coffee pot on top. Clay Art. Hand painted. Circa 1994. Made in China. $25.00.

CONDIMENT SETS

Condiment sets are among my favorites. Nodding shakers rest in the base with a compartment for the jar, lid, and a small serving spoon also. Frequently these sets are incomplete because the lid or spoon is missing.

Plate 424. Frolicking orange puppy and black bear cub play on a swing, 3½". Made in Japan. Impressed mark. $25.00 – 35.00.

Plate 426. Chicken condiment set. There are two other color variations. Note: a yellow baby chick is the lid's handle of this mustard pot. $75.00 – 90.00.

Plate 427. Brilliant parrots with mustard pot and ladle. Souvenir marked Patent T.T. $95.00.

Plate 429. Colorful chickens with mustard pot and ladle. Souvenir from Occupied Japan. $75.00 – 100.00.

Plate 428. Bluebirds sitting on an ornate tree branch beside a lidded pot with spoon. Mark: three-leaf clover in victory wreath. Japan. $100.00 – 150.00.

Plate 430. A pair of colorful chickens nod on a Satsuma condiment base. $75.00 – 125.00.

Plate 431. White glazed set of chickens with gilt trim. Mustard pot and ladle. Patent T.T. $75.00 – 100.00.

Plates 432, 433, and 434. Mexican souvenir condiment sets featuring the nodding matador and bull or matador with the señorita. Sets are complete with condiment lid and spoon. Japan with Patent T.T. mark. $100.00 – 175.00 each set.

Plate 435. Race horses with jockeys up, 2" x 5". Condiment set complete. Mark: three-leaf clover with semi-circle garland of leaves with a bow. Pat. K.S. on base. Japan. $75.00 – 150.00.

Plate 437. Two sets of Indian braves and shy squaws nod in baskets. Paper sticker. Japan. Patent T.T. $75.00 – 100.00 each set.

PEOPLE

Plate 436. Chinese mandarin and his lady nod yes. The applied three claw dragon is chasing a flaming pearl around the moriage base. A sea captain who lived on the shores of Lake Huron returned home with this souvenir for his wife. $300.00 – 400.00.

Plate 438. T'is said, this frightened couple are about to go over Niagara Falls in the barrel. Nod yes. Patent T.T. $75.00 – 90.00.

Plate 439. Another couple with Pennsylvania Dutch advice, "Ve get too soon oldt und too late Schmart." Of course they nod no. Patent T.T. $85.00 – 100.00.

Plates 441 and 442. Gray-haired black nodder photographed with and without her slice of watermelon. $225.00 – 250.00 each.

Plate 440. A courting Irish couple nod together on a porcelain base depicting the scene of "Upper Lake Killarney," 3½". Inscription reads "An tSeapain Tir a Dneanta." Translated, Made in Japan. Impressed PATENT T.T. on the base. $100.00 – 150.00.

Plates 443 and 444. A pair of brown nodders seated, arms outstretched, each holding a slice of watermelon. Yes heads nod for salt. The melon slice is for pepper. The man wears tribal sack cloth with body paint. The lady wears nothing. Made in Japan. Patent T.T. $225.00 – 250.00 each.

Plate 445. Rock 'n roll kids, 6". Holt-Howard sets with a paper label was produced in Japan but marketed in the United States. Circa 1959. $45.00 – 75.00 pair.

Plate 446. Skulls of several sizes and colors rest in the common square base. Prominent gold eyes and chattering teeth add interest and amusement. Patent T.T. White, $40.00 – 65.00. Purple, $35.00.

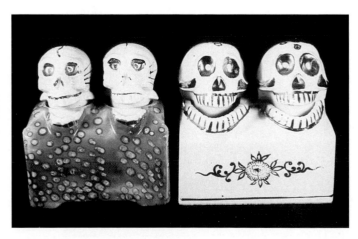

ANIMALS, FISH, AND FEATHERED FRIENDS

Plate 447. Parrot and woodpecker salt and pepper shakers painted and fired porcelain, 5½". Outstanding and rare, in excellent condition. Mold No. 5551 and 5552. Early 1900s. Germany. $300.00+ pair.

Plate 448. Horses gallop in a long box marked "Salt" and "Pepper." Patent T.T. $80.00.

Plate 449. Nodding donkeys rest in a square base. Made in Japan. Patent T.T. $45.00 – 60.00.

Plate 450. Kittens nod in a long box decorated with roses. They nod no. Paper labels, "A Quality Product Japan" and Patent T.T. $30.00 – 55.00.

Plate 451. The silly monkeys. $40.00 – 60.00.

Plate 452. A cute pair of young fawns. $30.00 – 40.00.

Plates 453 and 454. Bear cubs, sitting and standing, nod in similar decorated boxes. Made in Japan. Patent T.T. $35.00.

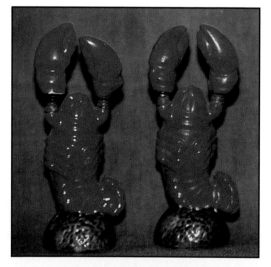 

Plates 455 and 456. Front and back view of lobster shakers resting on green seaweed. Paper sticker, an open scroll, "Our Own Import." Japan. $35.00 – 50.00.

Plate 457. Miniature salt and pepper penguins are photographed actual size, 2" x 1½". They are porcelain of exceptional quality, handmade by Carl and Laura Urban. (Laura is the artist-painter.) Signed on the post by Laura and on the base numbered 28 of 35 cast, circa 1994, C.D. Urban, Thomson, Illinois. The Urbans have been making these miniatures since 1992 and try to add several new ones each year. $50.00.

Plate 458. Pair of swans. $50.00.

Plate 459. Turkey gobbler and hen. $45.00 – 60.00.

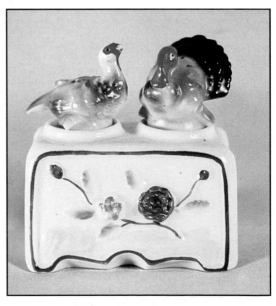

Plate 460. Pair of pheasants. $50.00.

Plate 461. Pair of chickens, all nod in square decorated boxes. Patent T.T. $50.00 –75.00.

Plate 462. Another hen and rooster nod on a stump with flowers growing around it. Mark, brown underglaze wreath of leaves encircling a three-leaf clover. Japan. $50.00 – 75.00.

Plate 463. Rock-a-bye bluebirds. $15.00.

Plate 464. The yellow canaries sing and swing from tree branches. Japan with mark. $15.00.

Plate 465. Baby chicks emerge from their eggshells. Left is ceramic. Right is plastic. They are a 1990 export from China. They rock on broken shells and appear identical until more closely examined. Plastic, $45.00. Ceramic, $65.00 – 100.00.

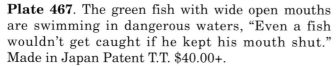

Plate 466. Trout and carp swim and nod with the sailboats. Japan Patent T.T. Fish, $35.00 – 50.00 each. Boat, $65.00.

Plate 467. The green fish with wide open mouths are swimming in dangerous waters, "Even a fish wouldn't get caught if he kept his mouth shut." Made in Japan Patent T.T. $40.00+.

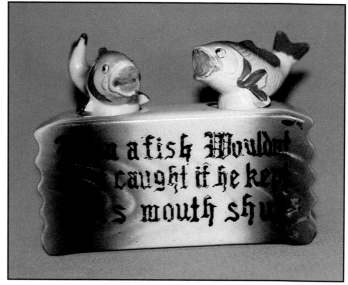

Plates 468 and 469. Raisin nodders from the 3rd Annual Michigan Convention. Available to members in attendance @ $25 per set. 5" tall. July 1988. $350.00+.

Plate 470. First Anniversary Michigan Commemorative shaker in rectangular base. Black (pepper) and white (salt) automobiles with platinum bumpers rock on Mackinac Bridge viewed in the background. Mark: a pair of wolf paw prints from K. Wolf Studios. Glazed pottery. Michigan Salt and Pepper Chapter. Circa 1990. $100.00+.

Plate 471. "A Nod to Abe," souvenir shaker from the 1991 annual Salt and Pepper Convention in Schaumburg, Illinois. Abe's top hat is 5¼", the girl is 3¾", the kneeling lad, 3½". Designed by Betty Harrington, designer for Ceramic Arts Studio, Madison, Wisconsin. Four hundred sets were produced by the Regal China Corporation USA. Their business ceased in June, 1992. $350.00+.

Santa Claus is ageless and over the centuries his transformation changed from solemn and stern to jolly and fashionable.

He began as the Bishop of Myra and lived in Asia Minor during the fourth century A.D. He was known as St. Nicholas, a renowned patron saint of Russia and protector of children. Riding his white horse, wearing a white embroidered robe, his annual visits throughout the countryside were a welcome sight. The resonance of his hand bell announced his arrival as he distributed gifts to the needy.

St. Nicholas Day evolved from this legacy, a tradition still celebrated on December 6th throughout much of Europe. On this special day St. Nicholas visits young children, good ones receive a present and the naughty are rewarded with a hickory switch.

His name also changed – on the Continent he was Pere Noel to French children, Sinter Claes to the Dutch, Weihnachtsmann in Germany, and Father Christmas in England. He became known as Kris Kringle in the United States by 1900, and Pelznickel to the Pennsylvania Dutch children. The style of his long cloak changed with colors – white, brown, blue, and green, to his more familiar red suit.

Christmas evokes memories of "chestnuts roasting by an open fire and Jack Frost nipping at your nose." Lyrics tell of Rudolf lighting the way bringing Santa from the North Pole to the top of the house and down the chimney.

Other times Santa arrived on his trusty steed, or by car, on skis, in a boat, or the modern-day airplane. But arrive he did.

Today's Santa is a fat, jolly old gentleman in a red velvet suit trimmed with fluffy white fur and carrying a bag of presents. His presence excites little people whether or not he arrives with the help of Rudolf.

Plate 472. Santa Claus is a special nodder bell, designed, sculptured, and handmade by the "Lost Wax" method and cast in highest quality bronze. 5½" (14cm). Created by Gerry Ballantyne of Overland Park, Kansas. Limited Edition No. 197 of 300 bells. Circa 1989. Ballantyne nodder bells are also discussed in Buddahs, Pagods, and Magots. ©Gerry Ballantyne. $300.00.

Plate 473. Santa has arrived with twinkling eyes, sitting in snow on top of the chimney and reflecting on gifts to be left below, 5¾". His head cheerfully bounces on a strong neck spring. He is also a money box. Vcago ceramics. Japan. $50.00 – 75.00.

Plate 474. Santa's coy little reindeer have plopped down for a rest, 5½". Plastic bobbin' heads, one is enameled, the other is flocked. Japan. $45.00 each.

Plate 475. Ceramic Santas are whimsical bobbin head nodders, 5½". "Made in Japan." Circa 1950s. $30.00 each.

Plates 476 and 477. This Santa is painted and fired bisque, 7½". There is no pin, rather his balancing act is on the pointed shaft that permits his body to sway and rotate. Santa was purchased from a gift shop in 1985. A Taiwan import. $75.00.

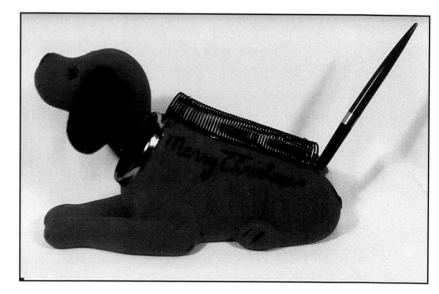

Plates 478 and 479. A laden Santa, 7½" x 6¾", and cute Dachshund puppy, 8" x 4¾", are both head hangers. They were patron gifts from a bank to loyal customers. Their wish to all is "Merry Christmas." Santa's back is stooped from the heavy money sack and spiral card holder across his back. The green-eyed puppy holds a convenient writing pen and the spiral on his back was for stamps. Naturally the money slot was intended for saving coins. $30.00 – 60.00 each.

Plate 480. Colorful papier-mâché Santa with a big red nose and a spring in his body, 5½". Paper label. A Rumpus Room Original, by St. Pierre & Patterson. Japan. $35.00 – 65.00.

Plate 481. Bisque Santa knotter is resplendent in his traditional fur trimmed suit and holding a sprig of box-wood, 2¾". Germany. $250.00+.

Plate 482. Miniature enameled wooden whimsy, 2¾". Photo is life size. Santa shakes his head on a spring and swings the lantern in his hand. This was a dime store trinket. Circa 1950s. Japan. $12.00 –15.00.

Plate 483. Glancing rock 'n roll Santa heads, 6". Salt and pepper shakers. Paper label of Holt-Howard. Grant Holt and John W. Howard started this company in Stamford, Connecticut, in 1949. Their unique designs were then manufactured in Japan. Kay Dee Design purchased the firm in 1990. Circa 1959. $45.00 – 75.00.

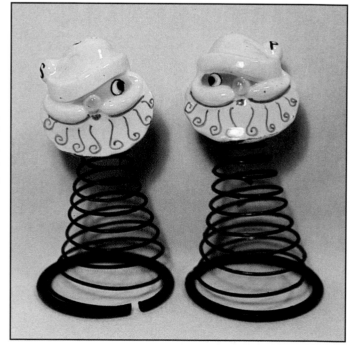

Plate 484. This plastic Santa is versatile, 4⅝". Hang him on your tree or if you prefer, anchor him by his boots with the suction cup in one of three positions on your table, against the wall, or in the window. Slight encouragement sets him swaying from the bottom of his boots. Japan. Post WWII. $15.00 – 25.00.

Plate 485. Santa has many helpers like this small elf holding a bottle brush Christmas tree, 4". He vigorously shakes his jolly head. This is one of a variety of plastic novelties marked BREBA. Early pieces were marked "Made in Germany," then "Made in Western Germany," and now "Germany." He came from the 1994 Kris Kringle Market in Nuremburg. $12.00 – 15.00.

Plate 486. That delightful little Snoopy is in a holiday mood, 3". Painted papier-mâché bobbin' head. Paper label, United Feature Syndicate, Inc. Circa 1958. $125.00.

Plate 487. A wiggly-head snowman appears to be jumping rope, 3½". Directions on the box: "If you tap this ornament gently, you'll see the snowman's head wiggle and jiggle! He's just the fellow to make you giggle this Christmas!" Product of China in molded plastic. Circa 1989. Hallmark introduced a line of hand-crafted Keepsake Ornaments in 1973. They became so popular a Keepsake Ornament Club was formed in 1987. Original cost of the snowman was $6.75. $24.00.

Plates 488 and 489. Clip-on ornaments of hand-blown glass are a German tradition. Ornaments with spring movement, like the peacock, have survived and are very collectible. Spring ornaments were also blown into fruits, animals, Santas, etc. Some were placed upright on spring clips, others suspended from tree branches. $25.00 – 75.00 each.

CHRISTMAS CANDY CONTAINERS

Christmas stockings hung by the fire were filled to the brim with toys. Candy containers held an assortment of tasty treats. Some have survived.

The candy box of early containers was quite small and the few pieces therein were a special treat.

By the 1930s Santa's hat and that of his helpers took on a conical shape but as far as children were concerned, Santa's hat was not a dunce cap. With the war, plastic appeared. Colorful pressed cardboard candy containers held their market share and were eye appealing, especially those with movement. These once inexpensive novelties are today's collectibles. Not all were imports, some were made in America.

Candy containers printed "U.S. Zone Germany" are from the Federal Republic of Germany occupation years, 1946 – 1949. They were popular with returning servicemen. After 1949 the mark read "Made in Western Germany." Since reunufucatuion the present mark is "Germany."

Plate 490. A plaster of Paris figure of Santa Claus standing on a small pressed cardboard box, 4¼". He nods from a spring in his neck. Germany early 1900. $250.00+.

Plate 491. The white polar bear is standing on a mica coated snowball that held a rather generous amount of candy, 4¼". It is wood-pulp-glue construction and the bear's head gives a vigorous nod from the steel strap in his neck. Pre WWI Germany. Original cost was $3.20. $375.00 – 425.00.

Plate 492. Eskimo girl with fur encircling her styrofoam head, 8". She rests on a beaded mica (candy box) block of ice. Paper label, "Made in Germany." $50.00.

Plate 493. This smiling red-nosed sprite once cost 49¢, 6½". Painted pressed cardboard. Arms are felt and his cotton beard conceals a spring coil neck. "Germany" stamped on base. Pre-World War II. $40.00.

Plate 494. A more serious elf is painted bright yellow, sprinkled with gold mica, and trimmed in red, 9". His mustache and full beard are rabbit fur and he stands in big black boots. Pressed cardboard, very good condition. Germany. $40.00 – 50.00.

Plate 495. A fine group of pressed cardboard snowmen, mica coated. Sizes range from 5¾" to 6½". One carries an umbrella, another wears a red top hat, another the black top hat with a hickory switch, and one snowman is a clown. All have a prominent bulbous nose and came from Germany. $35.00 – 75.00 each.

Plate 496. A snowman on long spring legs stands on his own candy box, 6¼". He looks festive with a big red crepe paper bow tie and black top hat. Made in Germany. $35.00.

Plate 497. This Santa's helper arrived on skis carrying a hickory switch, 7". He dates from the German occupation period, perhaps forewarning naughty children. He has a rabbit fur beard and bulbous nose, and his price tag was 69¢. $50.00 as is.

Plate 498. Nodding Santa and nodding reindeer, 10". A bell is on the tip of Santa's cap and his beard is cotton. He is covered with mica flakes and his pressed cardboard body held a generous amount of candy. Santa is from Germany, but the plastic reindeer, 5¾" x 4", are unmarked. Santa, $50.00. Reindeer, $20.00 – 30.00 each.

Plate 499. Santa's bulging abdomen is flocked pressed cardboard, 6¼". A rabbit fur beard outlines this jolly face and his cap sparkles with mica chips. Western Germany. $85.00.

Plate 500. The child who received this colorful container was lucky because it held a bounty of treats. Santa is 12" high. He holds a green fir sprig and the pressed cardboard is covered with mica flakes trimmed with a white garland. Mustache and beard are rabbit fur. Made in Western Germany. $60.00.

Plate 501. Not to be ignored is the hot pink Santa with a thick rabbit fur beard, 8". His pipe cleaner hands hold a tree branch. Mint condition. "Containers Made in Western Germany." 1960s. $50.00 – 85.00.

Plate 502. This Santa brought his own message, 7½". Germany. He sold for 79¢. $35.00 – 50.00.

Plate 503. The angelic choir girl is pressed cardboard and held a fair amount of treats, 7". The staples that connected her body parts are visible from the inside, but coated on the outside with red flocking. She is quite attractive with her white muff and top hat and condition is excellent. "Container Made in Western Germany." $25.00.

Plate 504. Choir boy holding a golden book of Christmas carols. His body is pressed cardboard, painted, and sprayed with gold glitter. Germany. Circa 1960s. Earliest use of this type of glitter coating was during the Depression. $45.00.

EASTER CANDY and OTHER CONTAINERS

Plate 505. When the head of this Plymouth Rock hen was removed she held only a small amount of candy, 3½". Sandy textured papier-mâché was molded and dipped in a plastic coating, then painted. The cocky rooster with coil spring legs is standing on a log, 4¼". Composition. On the bottom of the container written in pencil, "by August" and dated, April 1923. Hen, $175.00+. Rooster, $200.00+.

Plate 506. Papier-mâché duck standing on a round candy box, 5⅝". Wooden pencil stick from duck's body supports the coil spring inside its head. "Made in Germany" Early 1900. Circa 1920s $75.00 – 125.00.

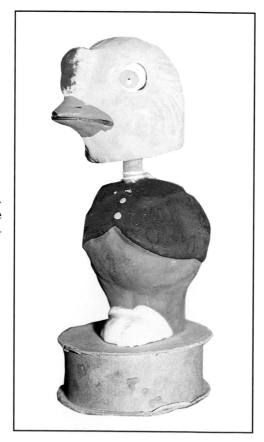

Plate 507. Two early 1900 papier-mâché ducks. The anthropomorphic girl duck's head bounces on a strong spring, 5½". The more innocent duck with a long beak swings his head via wires on the stick from his body, 5". Neither is a candy container. $75.00 – 100.00.

Plate 508. Yellow chick candy container with open beak, 6½". Pressed cardboard sprayed with beaded mica. "Made in Germany U.S. Zone." Circa 1947. $95.00.

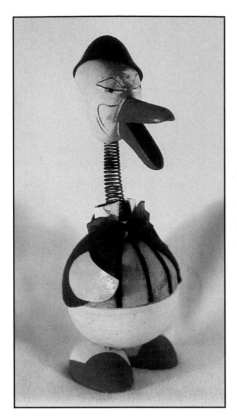

Plate 509. Many moons ago the Easter bunny delivered this duck with an elongated coil neck to a little girl named Cindy, 9¼". Cindy graciously added her quacky duck to my collection. Her mother recalled the original cost was $2.00, without the candy. Germany. Circa 1950s. $30.00 – 45.00.

Plate 510. Silly duck with spring neck, 8¼". The see-through nest of green grass once held candy eggs. Owner said from Germany, but paper sticker was missing. Post-World War II. $15.00 – 25.00.

Plates 511 and 512. Painted and fired bisque. Four dressed fowls wear gay finery. One child rides a hen, another sits on a rooster, the chick has a sore throat wrapped in a blue scarf, and the saucy rooster is dressed for an outing. The undressed fowls just wear their fine feathers. The crowing rooster is fine transparent porcelain, the others are painted and fired bisque. They stand on spring legs and bounce with slight encouragement. These miniatures, sometimes used as cake toppers, were imported from Germany. $90.00 – 125.00 each.

Plate 512. Mama goose and the gander on spring legs stand guard over two little goslings. Easter favors were sold in dime stores and groupings such as these were frequent cake-top decoration. They are ink stamped or printed GERMANY in raised letters. Pre WWII. $95.00 – 115.00.

Plate 514. Enameled white rabbits with spring necks, 7". "Made in Korea." Contemporary. $10.00 – 15.00 per pair.

Plate 515. Maybe this rabbit thought he was a chicken coming out of that egg, 6¾". He nods a long time from an inside metal weight. Not a candy container. $400.00+.

Plate 516. Eyes of the lamb and bunny are glass and their natural flocking would fascinate any child. Both are head hangers counterbalanced with a heavy weight in the neck. Paper label "Norleans" Japan. Post WWII. $65.00 each.

Plate 517. The pink rabbit with a coil spring neck is fragile chalkware that has been damaged, 5". Post WWII. $30.00 as is.

Plate 518. "Colorful Easter Egg Collectible," 3¾". Bobbin' head chick emerging from an eggshell supported by three rabbits hugging the shell. Top of eggshell forms umbrella over the chick. Plaster of Paris. Paper label, Made in China. Circa 1995. $5.00 – 8.00.

BIRTHDAY and ALL OCCASION CANDY CONTAINERS

Plate 519. Imagine a child's glee to find the little pig wearing a black top hat with lighted candle at a birthday party, 6". The solid figurine is well balanced and stands on the candy box. Germany, early 1900. $350.00.

Plate 520. The glass-eyed St. Bernard has a rider, 5" x 5½". The man's head nods while the dog's ears and tail quiver from a steel strap inside its body. Wood-pulp-glue composition dipped in plastic coating and painted, and papier-mâché construction for the dog. Separating the dog's neck reveals the candy container. From Germany, 1890, possibly earlier. $900.00+.

Plate 521. More German humor. The butcher sitting astride his pig nods yes and shakes a threatening knife over its head, 5" x 5½". Simultaneously the frightened pig's ears and tail quiver. This is a candy container when the pig's head is removed. Wood-pulp-glue composition. Late 1800. $1,025.00+.

Plate 522. This tricky magician is emerging from an eggshell, 6". Heavy brows, bulging eyes, and villainous look may be anticipating shenanigans. He convincingly nods yes from the wooden stick in his body to the connecting wires inside his head. His wood-pulp-glue construction places him at the turn of the century from Germany. Candy container. $400.00+.

Plate 523. This pleasant lad with hands folded on his knees nods yes, 5". His eggshell seat is another candy container. Turn of the century from Germany. $100.00 – 150.00.

Plate 524. The yellow frog's eyes bulge as he crawls out of the eggshell. The rider is dressed as a clown and holds a whip. Removing the frog's head reveals the container for candy. Composition. Rare, from Germany. $1,000.00+.

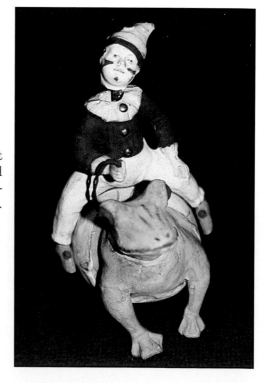

Plate 525. Wooly poodle dog candy container with spoiled Baby Snookums in the saddle. Poodle is carved wood, the body covered with lamb's wool. Snookums is composition and his silly head nods via a steel strap connecting head and body. Snookums is the strange looking kid of two doting parents referred to as dovey and precious from George McManus' strip The Newlyweds. Rare. Germany. $900.00+.

Plate 526. Baseball kid candy container, 6¼". Mica coated white baseball uniform and blue bill cap. In used condition. Ball in one hand, glove in other. Federal Republic of Germany between 1946 and mid-1949. $75.00 – 100.00 as is.

FOURTH OF JULY

Plate 527. Uncle Sam astride a firecracker and the wick's tip has been ignited. Pull on the burning wick to open the candy container. Composition. Rare, from Germany. $1,200.00+.

Plate 528. The anthropomorphic donkey promoting the National Democratic Convention. With an American flag around his neck he could be raising funds to fill his money box. Two white-gloved fingers are raised in "V" for Victory. $45.00 – 65.00.

HALLOWEEN

Plate 529. Full figure skeleton bobbin' head, 5¼". Unusual. Wood-pulp-glue composition dipped in wax and painted. Germany, early 1900. $150.00.

Plate 530. Hissing humped-back cat with tail held high, 2¾" x 2¾". Celluloid head hanger, attached at the nape with a cotton cord. Dime store item. $8.00 – 12.00.

Plate 531. Grinning goblins with a Pinocchio nose, 4¼". The ghoul's stone ax reads "Dirty old men need love, too." The witch thinks "We need each other." Amber glass eyes, fake wig, and furry tail. Semi-hard rubber construction with heads that turn and nod via flexible steel strap inside the body. No. 281, Made in Hong Kong. "It's the Berries" © 1971–72. $25.00 each.

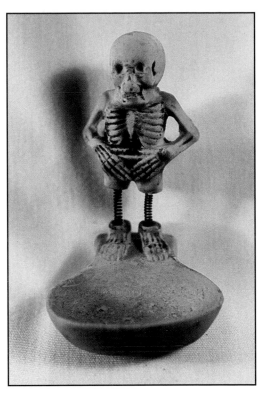

Plate 533. Spring legs of a bony skeleton rock on a green pintray, 3¼". Bisque. Made in Japan. Post WWII. $50.00 – 75.00.

Plate 532. Skeleton skull with wagging jaw is draped in black on the orange ashtray well, 3¼" x 4½". Glazed bisque, near mint condition but not a fine piece of art. "Made in Japan." $100.00.

Plate 534. Painted pottery duck dressed in an orange clown suit, holding a tambourine, 5¼". Strong neck spring. "Made in Japan," but very good copy from a German original. $65.00 – 90.00.

THANKSGIVING

Plate 535. Turkey gobbler bobbing on coiled legs atop the pumpkin candy container, 4½". Sandy plaster of Paris composition, realistically painted. Dates between WWI and WWII. Germany. $200.00+.

Plate 537. The papier-mâché pilgrim is so frightened his head shakes violently, 5¼". There is a magnet under his feet. No marks. $50.00 – 60.00.

Plate 536. Caricature of a papier-mâché pumpkin head wearing a funny hat, 5". Hole in corner of mouth held a cigarette. Spring inside head attached via a stick. Early 1900. "Made in Germany." $75.00 as is.

Plate 538. Pilgrim couple, 4½". Enameled wood components glued together. Spring neck supports their small heads. She holds the turkey and he wears the apron. $25.00.

Folk artisans produced their own unique form of art. They were talented craftsmen, self-taught without formal training. Their appealing work richly exemplified their heritage and lifestyle. Using materials at hand they created one-of-a-kind handmade objects using a variety of mediums. Perhaps papier-mâché was convenient but not durable compared to other crafts — carving, sculpting, quilting, painting, and weaving furniture from reeds and grasses. Some artisans are recognized for their work, but much was unmarked and remains anonymous, specifically the charming animated nodding figurines in papier-mâché that intrigue the nodder collector.

Although the art of wicker work dates back to ancient Egypt, during the mid-nineteenth century this popular fad was incorporated in the work of folk artists. Wicker furniture was popular. It was made of bent oak and hickory, often wrapped with stems, strong and serviceable. Seats were of woven reeds or of solid poplar and hickory wood padded with comfortable cushions. Relaxing on the porch was a fashionable Victorian pastime. Major retailers, such as Marshall Fields, advertised and marketed wicker furniture. In its heyday it is no surprise an idea for folk art nodders made an appearance. Although our nodder furniture is of crude construction it is symbolic of the times. Papier-mâché people were portrayed as they routinely conducted daily activities.

Although of minimal worth when they were created, these nodding caricatures had a human touch and a number of them have survived. Today they are pricey, cherished for their charm, and indeed collectible. They are fragile and sometimes firmly secured on a solid base. They are best displayed under glass domes or behind glass doors. Seniors seem to have been popular subjects with their balding hairlines, gray hair, and wire-rim granny glasses.

Plate 539. The parson and his wife in retirement, 5". An excellent pair of folk art yes nodders from the latter half of the nineteenth century. $500.00 pair.

The privilege of uniting this couple was a coincidence. My wonderful traveling friends also enjoy the hunt for my nodders. On their recent antiquing trip in England they found the parson sitting in his twig chair at an antique shop in Suffolk. They sent him home and he was to remain sequestered until Christmas to reappear under the Christmas tree. However, knowing my endeavor to place this manuscript in the hands of my publisher in the near future, their intuitive instinct prompted an early Christmas gift for this chapter.

To our amazement, at home on my shelf for nigh on five years, the parson's wife had been waiting. A happy happenstance!

The parson sits with his cane. His severe black suit is styled with a long coat. Knee britches meet the stockings below his knees and patent leather slippers are on his feet. His wife's expression is rather stern. Her cap is topped with a red bow and her blue polka-dot calico dress is floor length. She is holding a cup and saucer in her lap.

Folk art nodders from the mid-nineteenth century are not always in great condition. Fortunate finds such as these had to have been carefully preserved from moisture and damage.

Plate 540. This plate is best described by the lady who originally owned and cherished this nodder. Her letter to me compared the nodder to that of "a well used book, all there but evidently used." For many years the owner had carefully displayed it in a glass case among the laces in her New Orleans notion shop.

The nodder is a little white-haired lady with wire rim glasses relaxing on the wooden seat of her platform rocker, 5". Properly adjusted she nods a long time from the zinc weight inside her body. Her floor-length calico dress has a generous shawl collar. Papier-mâché. $300.00 – 375.00.

Plate 541 and 542. They are not a matched pair but an interesting couple and similar to the parson and his lady. The man's stern expression and erect posture in the overstuffed chair portrays him as a proper disciplinarian, 5½". He is wearing a severe black suit, the white cravat tied under his chin. His calf-length boots of soft leather were appropriate daytime attire in the 1880s.

The little old lady in wire-rim glasses nods her head sitting in her rustic chair, 3¾". Her worn condition has deteriorated with her age. Both are papier-mâché. $75.00 – 100.00 each, as is.

Plate 543. This papier-mâché couple are on a seat that is a hideaway for their jewels, 7" x 7". Drawers for jewelry open from either side and are slightly ajar as noted in the photo. Years have been unkind to this outstanding piece. The lady was probably knitting a stocking (missing) and the holds a woven basket. The present owner acquired this unusual set many years ago because the previous owner needed money for a dentist bill. No price available.

Plates 544 and 545. A colorful country couple are routinely tripping to market with their wares, 9". He trudges along with stick in hand, and totes baskets and a wooden-frame backpack. She carries her basket and a big black umbrella. Heads nod but she is doing all the talking because her lower jaw is jabbering as she walks beside him. $650.00 pair.

Plates 546 and 547. Beautiful bride and handsome bridegroom on their wedding day. The young maharajah and his lady are triple swayers, astride fine white horses, 12". Movement of the swaying horses sets the couple's head and torso in motion. This colorful pair came from the estate of a retired military officer who acquired them during a tour of duty in India. Circa 1920. $325.00.

Plate 548. Purchased at Kris Kindl Market, Frankfurt (Germany) airport. 23¾" tall. India, ca. 1994. $125.00.

Reproduction of colorful papier-mâché swayers, such as these, may be found in shops today. In Dec. 1994 the Kris Kindl Market at the Frankfurt (Germany) airport displayed a similar bride and groom among the artifacts from India, however quality and workmanship was not comparable to Plates 546 and 547.

Also in this booth were other swaying dancers. The dealer explained that they are temple dancers and their dress and jewels distinguish the country of their origin. These exotic dancers are colorful and elegant, quite charming but painted in watercolor that is easily damaged.

These swayers are made in four parts. The head rests on angled wires that support the upper torso which supports the rest of the body. This rests on a base. Properly adjusted the figurine is a three-way swayer.

Plate 549. Purchased at Kris Kindl Market, Frankfurt (Germany) airport. India, ca. 1994. 14½". $85.00.

Plate 550. Purchased at Kris Kindl Market, Frankfurt (Germany) airport. India, ca. 1994. 9¼". $65.00.

Plate 551. This is an earlier swayer, also papier-mâché, but better quality and painted in permanent oils. Doll enthusiasts collect these swayers and display them with their collections. Mid-1950s. $75.00.

Plate 552. Painted horse, 2½" x 4", stands on four delicate wooden legs. $125.00.

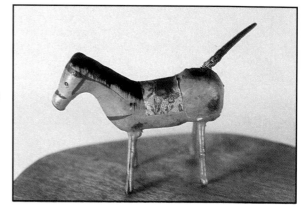

Plate 553. Black cat probably painted with water colors, 1½". The painted white puppy with has black spots, 2¼". $125.00 each.

These three composition animals have in common a lively spring tail. They were carried to the states from Switzerland in 1902 and presented as a gift to kinfolk here. Quaint and charming, they were of minimal value in their day. Possibly a cottage industry.

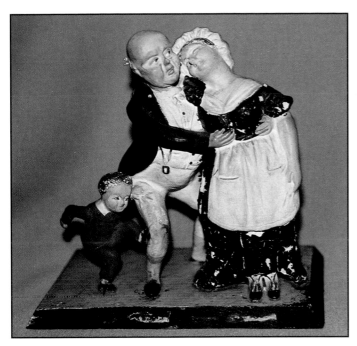

Plate 554. A humorous naughty scene in papier-mâché, 6½ x 5½". The lord of the manor affectionately embraces the kitchen maid. Resting her head on his shoulder with one arm around his waist, her expression is one of total bliss. However, the protesting young lord of the household made an unexpected appearance, grasping his father's pants leg and is poised for a swift kick. $350.00 as is.

Plate 555. Wooden Indian with a spring neck, 4". $2.50.

Plate 556. A wooden Asian dancer, 6½". She doesn't perform a real dance, but her expressive head on a spring neck tells it all. $5.00.

Plate 557. Wooden children springers. Pinochio, the fiddler, and the bowler, 3½". Japan. $7.50 each.

Plate 558. A trio of lively mountain men with concealed spring action in the neck make music with a bottle, drum, and guitar, 3¼". Their faces are hidden behind wire glasses, a ball nose, and rabbit fur beards. They are made of wood, rope, and burlap. $40.00.

Plate 559. On a recent flight to Denver my two granddaughters, Amanda and Ashley Irtz, surprised me with several nodders they made especially for my visit and are worthy of mention. Creative, yes, and they nod after a fashion. Their construction consists of paper cups, soda straws, toothpicks (in lieu of pins), shells, and a pine cone. Weights are silly putty and they are dressed in colorful felt clothes.

Now, who can top that! Priceless.

A true nodder is weighted. Bobbin' heads are not weighted. However, they are made in two or more parts and perform via a vibration or gentle touch from a spring or other mechanism inside the bobbin' head, activating this motion.

Materials are variable — ceramic, clay, plaster of Paris, papier-mâché, pressed cardboard, and composition. Many are easily damaged from careless handling and atmospheric conditions.

Clay is a substance from the earth, used by potters many years.

Plaster of Paris, a hard substance, is a compound mixture from calcined gypsum and water for casting small statuary. In appearance it closely resembles chalkware, a soft substance, easily damaged.

Papier-mâché, textually a "chewed paper," is a pressed and treated pulp-glue-oil-resin mixture that has been a plaything for all ages, as well as a popular source of nodder material. It is lightweight and strong, can be molded, decorated, and lacquered. The Chinese used this knowledge in ancient times.

Cardboard figures are molded or pressed between a male and female dye, then dipped or coated, and finished.

Composition bobbin' heads present an interesting background and imprecise definition. An aggregate of two or more elements must be combined, such as glue with pulp paper to form papier-mâché. A hollow papier-mâché head can be attached to the molded body with a coiled wire or other spring mechanism. Extensive use of this material gained popularity around the turn of the century. Butler Brothers advertised composition as being indestructible (not true), and it came into practical usage amidst a growing WWI anti-German sentiment. The products were boycotted well into the twentieth century until introduction of plastics around 1940.

The seven nodders in Plate 560 were purchased by the author at the annual Golden Glow Convention in August 1989. At this convention Christian Palmer gave an informative presentation on like composition figures. He noted that exact composition differed among manufacturers, but basically consisted of a variation of several ingredients — wood-flour, kaolin, animal glue, casein, and water. When pressed and dried, this produced a firm, sandy texture.

Palmer's paper on composition figures later appeared in the *Golden Glow©*, a newsletter dedicated to enthusiasts of Christmas antiques and collectibles. *Golden Glow©* is distributed to club members five times a year. Palmer pictured the interior differences between German and Japanese composition in Plates 561 and 562.

Plate 560. A tableau of nodders, 7". Left to right: Uncle Sam, Sambo, Foxy Grandpa, Rabbit, Happy Hooligan, Keystone Cop, and Alphonse. $3,500.00+ per set.

These composition nodders are early 1900, produced in Germany. Although not great works of art, caricatures are humorously portrayed as real or fictional, depicting culture from the turn of the century. The composition mold is anchored on a wood base and construction for producing movement is distinctive, neither weighted nor coiled. A pencil-thin stick secured inside the body cavity connects a wire mechanism within the head at the temples, consisting of a U-shaped wire curled on a cross wire. No external wires are visible, the head rests and nods. Most of these charming nodders have lively movement and are ink stamped "Germany" on the bottom.

Plate 561. Interior of a wooly sheep. Germany. Christopher and Jenny Palmer Collection. No price available.

Plate 562. Interior of a horse. Japan. Christopher and Jenny Palmer Collection. No price available.

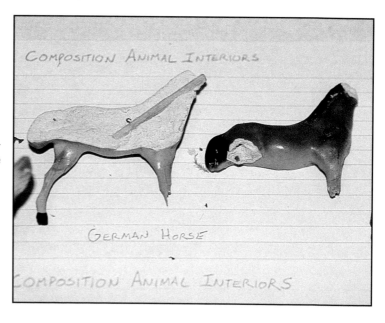

Palmer Cox Brownies are recognized with long spindly legs supporting their rotund body and head. Author-artist Palmer Cox, created popular Brownie characters for *St. Nicholas*, an illustrated magazine for young people. Antics of these popular characters delighted reading audiences in the 1880s and enjoyed world renown. Brownie figurines were popular from about 1890 to 1920. Germany.

Plate 563. Composition nodder with big eyes, 7". $250.00 – 375.00.

Plate 564. The black minstrel man, 7". $250.00 – 375.00.

Plate 565. Long-legged Happy Hooligan Brownie with a round body and red tin-can hat, 11¾". Pencil stick from body into head connects wire mechanism. $250.00 – 375.00.

Plate 566. French bellhop with nodding construction same as above, 6¼". His Pinocchio nose overshadows a grinning smile. Composition. Germany. $125.00 – 175.00 as is.

Plate 567. White haired country gentleman wearing a wide brim hat, 6". His big shaking head and that curly (real hair) goatee produce vigorous tremors. Original price was 75¢. "Made in Germany." Early 1900s. $250.00.

Plate 568. One-eyed character, nicknamed by his owner as the winkey one, 4¾". Later period than other nodders of this type. Papier-mâché head rests on a spring and wooden peg that is anchored inside the composition body. Germany. $150.00+.

Plate 570. Caricature of a Keystone Cop, 6¼". A small hat is perched on an enlarged head resting on knee-high boots. Similar nodding construction. Worn condition. Germany. $75.00 as is.

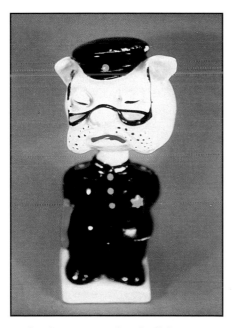

Plate 569. From his damaged condition he is truly a fighting Irishman. The lighted cigarette is not original, but he is still happy, 5½". Same nodding construction. Germany. $75.00 as is.

Plate 571. Anthropomorphic bulldog in policeman's uniform, 5". Pottery with neck spring. No marks. $22.00.

NOTABLES

Since the mid-twentieth century, contemporary papier-mâché, composition, and plastic bobbin' heads achieved an identity of their own. Action is produced from the coiled spring copied from earlier composition and papier-mâché nodders on the continent. A variety of bobbin' heads can be accumulated in this popular category. Many are recognized from real life as caricatures, comic characters, and animals. Artists from Japan copied copiously. More recently Taiwan, Hong Kong, Korea, and China exported bobbin' heads through syndicated American companies.

Plate 572. Colonel Harland Sanders, 1890 – 1990, of Kentucky Fried Chicken fame, 7". He seems to be saying, "It's finger-lickin' good." $75.00.

On September 9, 1990, the anniversary of the Colonel's 100th birthday, a celebration was held in Corbin, Kentucky, at the site of his original restaurant, restored and re-opened as a museum. The legend of Colonel Sanders and his famous secret recipe has spread to 59 countries throughout the world. A silver paper sticker on the base of this bobbin' head says "Chars Prod. Japan." The Colonel's daughter, Mildred Ruggles, tells me these bobbin' heads were token gifts to franchise owners in the 1950s. The distinguished Colonel with his familiar black walking stick holds his famous bucket of fried chicken. He is an imposing figure with heavy black-rim glasses, white Palm Beach suit, black string tie, and black shoes.

Plate 573. Two smiling Shriners resplendent in a tuxedo, bow tie, and fez, 6¾". Japan. $50.00 – 75.00.

Plate 574. Leo Carrillo, 1881 – 1961. Leo achieved popularity as a supporting actor in the 30s and 40s. His role was usually a Mexican or Latin cowboy, but he appeared in many musical comedies. His prominent moustache and 10 gallon hat graced many a movie screen as he chased the bad guys along with Johnny Mack Brown or Tom Mix. $45.00.

Plate 575. Kids looked forward to Saturday morning because "It's Howdy Doody Time." The program ran from 1947 to 1960. Buffalo Bob Smith was master of ceremonies. More than 600 manufacturers received permission to license and distribute this popular character and he is still around, evidenced by this nodder, circa 1988. 4" x 5". Howdy Doody is dressed in vivid colors and wearing his cowboy boots. This nodder was authorized by NBC and found in shops and auction houses. $25.00 – 45.00.

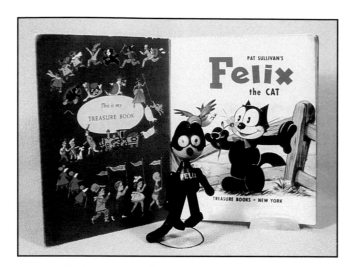

Plates 576 and 577. In 1920 Felix Cat was the first animated character, 4". He preceded Mickey Mouse by a decade. Three years after his introduction, the comic strip followed. Creator was Pat Sullivan who died an alcoholic in 1933 at the age of 48. In its heyday Felix's popularity rivaled other comedians like Charlie Chaplin and Buster Keeton. A. Schoenhut manufactured several sizes of Felix. $225.00+.

Plates 578. Peanuts Gang, 5". Left to right, Schroeder, Lucy, Charlie Brown, Snoopy, Linus, and Pig Pen. $50.00 – 125.00 each.

This popular comic strip written by Charles M. Schultz has delighted readers since 1950 and has been followed in more than 2,300 newspapers. Charlie Brown is still a little kid even though he is over 40 years old. The characters have been marketed in more than 300 different products, including motion pictures, plays, songs, radio and TV programs, greeting cards, toys, Christmas ornaments, clocks, and children's books to mention a few, and our delightful Charlie Brown gang of bobbin' heads. They are of papier-mâché composition construction and easily damaged with careless handling. Charlie Brown was a little daydreamer, the first Peanuts character to appear on the scene.

These are six original Peanuts bobbin' head gang members and were distributed by United Features Syndicate on October 2, 1950. A red and gold paper label on the base reads, "Fine Quality, Lego, Japan."

Plate 579. Smaller size Lucy and Charlie Brown in his blue cap, 3¾". Paper label Copr.© 1950. United Feature Syndicate, Inc. 3½". $80.00 per pair.

Plate 580. Snoopy the race car driver is at the wheel, 3½". Same copyright, circa 1986. Made in Korea. $125.00.

Plate 581. Woodstock, same copyright, circa 1965 and 1972. $85.00.

Plate 582. The Beatles were four talented young men from Liverpool, England. Their Pan Am flight from London arrived at Kennedy International Airport on February 7th, 1964, and created pandemonium that continued wherever they went. The foursome disbanded in 1974 but their popularity lives on. The papier-mâché bobbin' head Beatles are, from the left, John Lennon, Paul McCartney, Ringo Starr, and George Harrison, 7¼" to 8¼". © CAR MASCOTS, INC 1964. Made in Japan and marketed through Consolidated Sales Co. of Los Angeles, CA. Original cost was 97 cents each. Complete boxed sets could also be purchased, and if complete today including original box are pricey. $750.00+ set.

Plate 583. A smaller size of the Fab Four group, 3¾", topped the birthday cake of a young Beatles fan. These plastic bobbin' heads are recent, made in Hong Kong. $30.00 – 45.00 per set.

Plate 584. The big-eyed little fellow with pointed ears and spiky blue hair is a troll, 5½". Papier-mâché with a paper JAPAN label. Circa 1960s. $35.00 – 50.00.

During the 1960s trolls gained popularity in a variety of doll characters like this amusing little bobbin' head. A coil spring concealed inside the troll's head produces good movement. Troll dolls are found in souvenir and gift shops and considered good luck. Young children twirl their hair and make a wish. This nodding bobbin' head troll is the only one I have seen.

Plate 585. A whimsical bobbin' head American Indian with tomahawk. Papier-mâché. $200.00+.

Plate 586. Caricature of Canadian Mountie, 5¼". Spring neck. Canada souvenir, but "Made in Japan" stamped on base. $35.00.

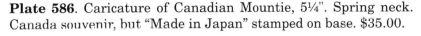

Plate 587. Black "Bahamian Policeman" souvenir of the Bahamas, 8½". Papier-mâché springer wearing a snappy uniform. Unmarked. $35.00.

Plate 588. Young soldier boy standing at attention with his bugle in hand. Dressed in a smart uniform. Strong spring neck. Pottery money box. $25.00.

Plate 589. Boys love to clown. The enameled clay bobbin' head holds a noisy horn, 7½". He was marketed by Wal-Mart, Bentonville, Arkansas. Paper label. Made in Taiwan R.O.C. Circa 1989.

The other kid, sticking out his tongue, wears a dark blue clown suit of enameled pressed cardboard, 8½". He was a booby prize at a telephone office Christmas party. Dated December 16, 1937. Made in Japan. $35.00 – 75.00 each.

SPORT MASCOTS

Fans have collected sports related bobbin' heads more than 40 years. Frequently they are referred to as bobbing head dolls. Originally sold in sports arenas for a nominal sum, interest and demand has escalated to astronomical prices for well-known celebrities from the 1960s. Not all mascots bear a like resemblance to the personality, perhaps only the uniform, name, or number is recognized. Early figurines were papier-mâché, imported from Japan by Sports Specialties, a Los Angeles company. A Swiss company, Lego, is another. Later they appeared in plastic from Taiwan, Hong Kong, and Korea. Recently papier-mâché is reappearing on the market.

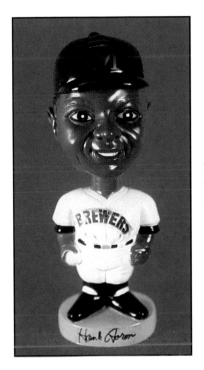

Plate 590. Hank Aaron played baseball in the major league from 1954 to 1976. He wears No. 44 on the back of his uniform. 7½". Taiwan. Circa 1974. Plastic. $300.00.

Plate 591. Cincinnati Reds baseball players. Left, 7", plastic. Korea. Circa 1974. Right, 6½", papier–mâché. Patent Pending. Japan. Circa 1961. White base, $400.00 – 600.00. Gold base, $75.00.

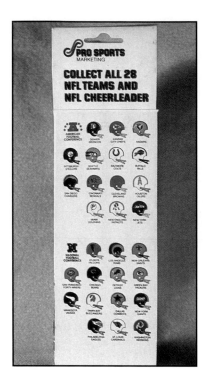

Plates 592 and 593. Pittsburgh Steelers No. 0 is running with the football, 8". NFL official licensed product, box label "Collect all 28 NFL Teams and NFL Cheerleader." Plastic. Made in Hong Kong. Back of Pro Sports box photographed. $40.00 with box.

Plate 594. NFL Green Bay Packers No. 00 holding his football, 8". Papier-mâché. Paper label, exclusive licensee, Sports Specialties L.A. 67 Calif. Japan © 1968. $45.00.

Plate 595. A basketball player from the Portland Trailblazers, 6½". Papier-mâché. Circa 1967 – 71. $100.00.

Plate 597. "Mini-Bobble Head Doll." These players represent the California Angels and Los Angeles Dodgers. Heads are on a spring. 3½". COLLECTIBLE TEAM product of SKORE ©MLB 1989. A Division of Eskor Industries Inc Larkspur, Ca 94939. Made in China. $5.00 each.

Plate 596. Seattle Supersonics basketball kid. Papier-mâché. Circa 1967 – 71. $45.00.

MISCELLANEOUS

Bobbin' heads proved to be a popular traveler's memento for folks back home. But as with most souvenirs, novelties retire, are forgotten, or discarded. Surviving specimens in malls and flea markets find ready buyers. Occasionally a money slot was included, but they are better appreciated for action, amusement, and collectibility.

Plate 598. The big-eared mouse standing by a pineapple is also a money box, 5¾". Paper label, Rosine. Japan. $25.00.

Plate 599. A Chippewa Indian girl money box from the Lac Du Flambeau Indian Reservation, 6". Plaster of Paris. This tribe lives in northern Wisconsin, a great area for spear fishing. A few years ago the Indians regained their fishing rights from an old treaty. The tribe has produced a variety of bobbin' heads. $30.00.

Plate 600. The irate golfer, 6½", says, "I only said Putt up." The frustrated bowler says, "Your right down my alley." Papier-mâché on a wood base. Paper label. A rumpus room original by St. Pierre and Patterson © Ca 1961 Japan. $35.00 each.

Plate 601. Chinese boy with pigtail and rhinestone eyes. A papier-mâché money box. Paper label. Korea. $45.00.

Plate 602. Impoverished hobo, 8½". Papier-mâché and composition on wood base. $25.00.

Plate 603. Caricature of a chubby business man, 4½". His inscription says, "Congratulations! Today was the day you were born." Paper label. Japan. $22.00.

Plate 604. The inebriated man insists, "I can't be all bad...they like me." Why else would he be cuddled by two baby elephants! Papier-mâché and composition. Paper label. Japan. $28.00.

Plate 605. Well-dressed Scotsman with handlebar moustache. Papier-mâché. $18.00 as is.

Plate 606. Confident young golfer with strong spring neck, 7". Golf clubs are strapped on his back and he is holding a tee in the corner of his mouth. $25.00.

Plate 607. Generic pair. He still sends glances her way. Paper label. VCAGCO Ceramics Japan. $45.00 pair.

CARTOON CHARACTERS

Modern Warner Bros. bobbin' heads are colorful, good quality, and a current inexpensive category of collectibles. They have a strong neck spring and were made in China of durable hard plastic.

Each character comes in a specially fitted box. The serious collector keeps original containers for additional value.

Plate 608. Marvin Martian, Yosemite Sam, Tweety, and Bugs Bunny are classic Looney Tunes bobbin' heads marketed through Disney stores. They range in size from 6½ to 8¾". Circa 1994. $15.00 each.

Plate 609. Bugs Bunny dressed for a game of golf. The Tasmanian Devil leans on his baseball bat. Made in China. Circa. 1993 – 1995. $15.00 each.

Plate 610. "Wedding Bliss," another Looney Tune, same construction, 8¾" x 7¾". The ornery Bugs Bunny finally gets a bride. TME© Warner Bros. Designed exclusively for the Warner Bros. store. 1994. $30.00.

Plate 611. Donald Duck, dressed in sailor blue, 5". Donald made his first appearance in "The Wise Little Hen" in 1934. By 1935 he appeared with Mickey Mouse in the first color cartoon, "The Band Concert." He has been performing ever since, a popular and irascible little duck. copyright WDP, made in USA. An Irwin toy, in Fitchburg, Massachusetts. $90.00 – 100.00.

Nodders in this chapter are so diversified that I categorize some as something else. They are novel and different, unusual or rare, but nodders they are. They are in pairs. They are whimsical. They are distinctively amusing. They are refreshing.

They are naughty. Quality ranges from fine art to mundane consequentials. But true to nodder connotation the movement must be activated by natural force, a vibration, breeze, or that gentle touch.

Plates 612, 613, and 614. A rare French brass thermometer, 8", weight 4 pounds. The nodding mandarin's open coat reveals a double reading of the thermometer scale. Back and side views of this handsome nodder have been photographed. Mark "FRERES." Price not available.

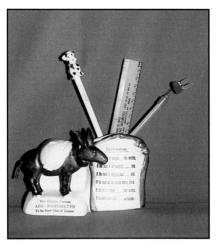

Plate 615. The top of your pencil is a good place for a nod, especially when resting inside a nodding-donkey barometer, 4¼" x 6". Barometer is marked "FOREIGN," of Japanese export made for sale outside of England, or for sale in England. Donkey, $150.00. Pencils, $1.00 each.

Plate 616. Have you ever seen a nodding doorstop? That is what this wrought iron donkey does, 10¼" x 12½". It is rather rare, of heavy cast iron weighing in at 13 lbs. Like an obstinate donkey, he nods slowly and is of unknown origin. From appearance, he has been kicked around. The grayish color is original, possibly applied at the foundry. $500.00.

A donkey has no understanding. He is not stubborn, but he is positive. He will not argue. He will move, or he won't until ready to pass his own judgement. The doorstop, or door porter, was a convenient door anchor for circulation of air throughout the house. This English innovation came into practical use in our country after the Civil War.

SCHÄFER & VATER WHIMSIES

In the late nineteenth century inexpensive novelties could be found in the average American home. Many were imported from Germany, humorous, whimsical, and today, very collectible.

They amused all ages. One manufactory, outstanding for small amusing figurals, is Schäfer & Vater Porzellanfabrik in Rudolstadt, Thuringia, Germany, recognized for whimsical and decorative porcelain figurines. The identification mark may be impressed but sometimes barely visible, or it may be recognized by the dis-tinction of the piece, or it may be completely void of any mark. Look for a multi-pointed star, sometimes an "R" within this star, and/or a three-pointed crown above, plus an occasional mold number.

This porcelain factory came into existence in 1890 and continued production until 1960. Movement is activated via a wire, often completely concealed. These whimsical novelties were frequently molded with an open container at the side or back of the figure. A wire in the temple area produces their nod.

Plate 617. A silly monkey offers a piece of fruit but shakes his head no, 4¼". Mold no. 7802. He is squatting beside an open tree stump and his condition, detail, and color are excellent. Shäfer & Vater mark. $300.00+.

Plate 619. Caricatures of two smiling ladies wearing bonnets on oversized heads, and nod affirmatively, 4½". Tea time with a cup and an open book. Mold no. 3391 and 6858. Excellent condition and marked Shäfer & Vater. $200.00 each.

Plate 618. Little pink pig sitting upright on his haunches, 3¾". His gleeful grin "Not your bacon" says he isn't a candidate for the hot tub. Excellent condition with Schäfer & Vater mark and mold no. 7508. $325.00 – 350.00.

Impressed Schäfer & Vater mark. No color.

Plate 620. Attractive blond(e) dressed in man's clothing and black top hat, nods yes, 5". She is somewhat problematic because one hand holds an envelope sealed with a red heart. She is an excellent nodder and her features are refined and delicate. Unmarked Shäfer & Vater. $200.00.

Plate 621. A balding pot-bellied gentleman bows, sways, and coyly extends his hand holding a rose, 4¾". He stands by a pin tray base in front of his top hat. The shirttail protruding from his coattail adds to his amusing appearance. Condition excellent. No mark but attributed to Shäfer & Vater. $225.00+.

Plate 623. She shouldn't be dusty because she is sweeping it away with her big broom, 4". Mold no. and mark are indistinct, but faded original price appears to have been 25 cents. Excellent condition and very collectible. Shäfer & Vater. $700.00 – 800.00.

Plate 624. A whimsical monk and bug-eyed friar, 4¼". The monk's head shakes but his tongue is frozen. Mold No. 1801 with faint mark. Holding the goblet and rubbing his belly says the wine is good. But the friar has an open book and thumbs up signal. Excellent condition and impressed Schäfer & Vater mark. $325.00+ each.

Plate 622. An Alpine musician, 4". Dressed in forest green and wearing his feathered loden hat, he yodels and strums his instrument. Excellent and marked Schäfer & Vater. $275.00+.

Plate 625. Frankensteins are look-alike twins, both with a tousled wig of real hair, 3½". The pugilist is dressed in bodytights with socks laced to his knees. Their counterweight is a lead ball. The basketball player in body suit is marked Germany with mold no. 9411. Both nod yes. They are excellent nodders despite their thinning hair and the balding forehead of the basketball player. $300.00+ each.

Plates 626 and 627. Seated Oriental lady, 5". The opening at her back was intended for an ashpot. Head swings on wire through the elongated neck. Brilliant yellow contrasts her black hair and gold tiara. Porcelain in excellent condition. Germany. Rare. $175.00 – 225.00.

Plates 628 and 629. Front and back views of two Oriental caricatures. Heads swing from flat wire pushed through elongated neck. The blue figurine is a pastille burner. A small opening for escaping smoke is visible inside the pointed neck and center of his hat. The other nodder is a match holder. These unusual and rare porcelains are from Germany. Circa 1891 – 1921. $225.00+ each.

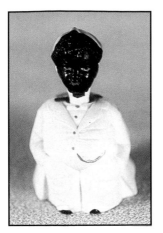

Plates 630, 631, and 632. A two-faced nodder is unusual and rare. He is Oriental, but turned around he is black, a clever little mold of translucent porcelain, 3½". Viewed full front, this nodding figurine conceals the secret behind him. His dual persona has been cast with one head on a single neck that nods yes on a body with two fronts. One front is a Chinese mandarin with almond eyes, brows, and Fu Manchu mustache. He is an official of lower rank, personified in colorful turquoise-lavender gilt, devoid of embellishments. A long strand of beads hangs from under his collar and appears draped across his lap under the opium pipe. He sits with feet crossed in the Oriental manner. Turned around is the squatty figure of a young black man with a head of thick kinky hair. An artist brushed a streak of black paint under this chin, neglecting most of the entire neck to match his face. He is neatly dressed in a yellow long-tail coat, white shirt, dangling gold watch chain, blue slacks, and black shoes. Hands are thrust in the pockets of this upright portly figure. A side view depicts two distinct portly bodies. The modeler adeptly molded, painted, and balanced a dual personality. One single flat pin pierces the neck and the bell-type clapper counterweight is bisque and cannot be removed through the aperture. Unmarked. Germany, late nineteenth century. $600.00.

Plate 633. Little girl is brushing her hair in front of her mirror. Painted bisque porcelain. She is rare and unusual, designed as a swayer and a place-card holder. Made in Germany. Later copies came from Japan. Private Collection. $100.00.

Plate 634. Three free spirits. Painted and fired bisque. Dangling legs push into their body cavity. The inebriated bum, 4", nods a pleasant affirmative via a wire through his temples as he nips from the bottle. Under his hat a hank of real hair falls behind his ears. 58/196 fired on the solid base in black ink. Bisque, possibly of German origin, however similarity to Ardalt nodders in The Far East Chapter is noted. Ardalt and several other manufactories in Japan exported wares of excellent quality to the English markets after WWII. The relaxed bum with handle-bar mustache and wearing a 1920s straw hat is cooling his inflamed feet. He is holding onto that long-stem pipe. The optimist with the "Racing Form, Everyday a Winner"...possibly, if he can keep that cigarette in his mouth, hold on to the bottle, and stay awake. $175.00+ each.

BOBBIN' HEADS FROM SPRING and WIRE MOVEMENT

Plate 636. Highly glazed twin clowns nod no from wings molded to the neck. Also a slot for coins. Origin uncertain, but new. The toothy clown with a broad grin wears a silly hat and nods yes from wire through his temple, 4½". The wing collar balances a global body that hides a match container behind him. Mold No. 1101. Possibly unmarked Shäfer & Vater. Twins, $45.00 each. Global, $175.00.

Plate 635. The clown holds the attention of a wobbly goose on spring legs, 4". The goose is in training. Painted and fired bisque. Germany. Mold No. 1853. $135.00.

Plate 637. President Clinton has put on boxing gloves and dressed for a workout, 9". Thus his head bounces easily from the spring in his neck but his arms must be adjusted manually. Circa 1994. $12.00.

Plate 638. A handy ceramic chef, 4" x 5" long. The chef's hat on his brown face complements his black and white suit shaped as a spoon holder. Marked © Geo. Z. Lefton #90413, signed J.C. Circa 1950 – 1955. George Lefton immigrated to the United States from Hungary in 1939, and the following year formed a company in Chicago. After WWII he imported ceramic gift-type items from the Far East. $100.00.

Plate 640. Campbell Kid, 10". Although the idea of a container for cookies originated abroad, in time it was destined to became a universal receptacle for special treats. This cookie jar has a happy-head lid with very lively bouncing action. Woe to any little thief who stole a cookie from his rotund body because the vigorous bobbing head was a dead give-away. Glazed pottery jar has some crazing. Publicity from the late Andy Warhol's vast collection of cookie jars brings this collectible category into prominence. Mark unidentified. Da V Ar. $75.00 – 100.00.

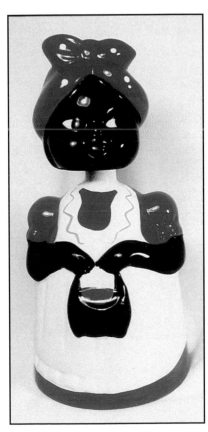

Plate 639. Neat young African American lady carrying a handbag, 8". She is highly glazed ceramic, new, and unmarked. Also a slot for coins. $25.00.

Plate 641. A jolly head cork stopper bounces up and down bringing attention to the contents of his bottle. These amusing stoppers were popular souvenirs of returning travelers and servicemen. Germany. $25.00.

PAIRS

Occasionally nodders are seen with a different type of pin. This threaded pin was fitted with screws to secure the movable parts in place for proper movement. Excellent quality of many of these figurines attributes them to German origin. Over the years, some of the holding screws have been lost and the threaded pin replaced, but collectors recognize certain characteristics. Nodders with this special pin are so noted.

Plates 642, 643, and 644. Several views of a swaying Bavarian couple, 6". A threaded neck pin with holding screws supports head, arms, and post counterweight all molded together to form the upper torso. Open sides of their bodies permit lively swaying motion. The man's Utopian glow and mug of beer is undeniable, but fräulein's expression is somber. Semi-translucent porcelain. This is a pre-WWII import that bears a partial paper label with legible (New) York. P & Co. Condition near mint. Origin uncertain. $500.00 – 575.00.

Plates 645 and 646. Happy-go-lucky elders signal with one and two fingers and place the other hand over on their heart, 6". They ride on a sphere with a gaping mouth and protruding lower lip. Eye glasses are molded to their face. Threaded pins with holding screws pierce the couple's waistline, affording lively back and forth movement. I had the old gentleman a long time and he was quite lonely until my friend, Ted Quell, graciously provided his mate. This typifies couples that have been separated over the years and reunited through happenstance. Let's keep our pairs together. Semi-transparent porcelain, near mint condition. Mid 1900s. $475.00.

Plates 647 and 648. Pig riders of the same period, 6". Two views. Pigs have been harnessed for a joy ride. These whimsies are fine semi-translucent porcelain. Post counterweights with threaded pins and holding screws pierce the neck and rest on the aperture. Grandpa's eyes send her a sly glance. Granny glasses are molded on the face. $475.00.

Plates 649 and 650. Boys see-saw on one candlestick; girls see-saw on the other one, 8¾". They are sturdy and quite elaborate with holders for two candles on each candlestick. Semi-translucent bisque painted in delicate pastels. $175.00 – 250.00.

Plate 651. Brother and sister in clown dress sit at the base of a pair of tree stump candlesticks, 7½". Semi-translucent bisque. Their heads nod from post counterweights. No marks. Early 1900. $150.00 – 200.00.

Plate 652. This single candlestick for two candles is balanced with a pair of monkeys at the center, 9¾". The candlestick is a glazed Staffordshire-type, but the monkeys are painted and fired bisque. $200.00 – 250.00.

WITTY NAUGHTIES

Plate 653. Hawaiian girl wearing a topless skirt doing the hula and nodding no, 6". The lei partially conceals her bare upper torso. Painted and fired ceramic with Ardalt crest numbered 6531. Post WWII Japan. $55.00.

SMOKING RELATED

Today cigarette smoking is banned many places. Thus accouterments of this latent habit are noteworthy. The common ashtray has become collectible, especially one with movement. Some of our nodders in questionable risque poses were abreast of the times. These are marked with Patent T.T, Japan, or Made in Japan, dating after 1921 up until World War II.

Plate 654. A flapper is getting her kicks in a decorated bathtub ashtray, 5½" x 5¼". A variety of these amusing ashtrays surface frequently in shops and at antique shows. $55.00 – 75.00.

Plates 655 and 656. Sunbathers on a daybed, 4¾" x 5¼". Ashes were deposited by milady's swinging legs, but an opening beneath her head was intended for the lighted cigarette. The design of this amusing feature permitted smoke from the smoldering cigarette to curl around her swinging legs and waving fan. $85.00 – 125.00.

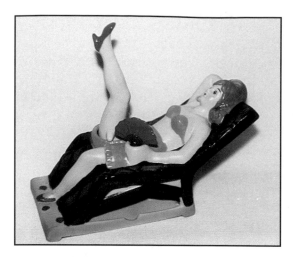

Plate 657. Lady on a reclining chair, 5¾" x 6". The depository for ashes is underneath. Smoke curls around her swinging leg and encircles the fan she holds in her left hand. Paper label, Made in Taiwan. Purchased from a catalog in 1984. Original cost was $6.50 plus shipping. $35.00 – 50.00.

Plate 659. The typewriter, what a great invention! This grinning fellow with a cigar in his mouth is pounding typewriter keys, 6½" x 4". Threaded pins with holding screws support his excellent nodding head and typing hands. A newspaper article from the 1930s reported that a pair of nodding typists were an eye-catching window display for an English typewriter firm. The first typewriter was patented June 23, 1868, and the article attributed the advertisement to early 1900s. No marks, possibly German. This was one of a pair, his lady companion is missing. $175.00 – 200.00.

Plate 658 Blonde lady wearing gold slippers, relaxed in a large lounge chair. $75.00+.

Plate 660. Old man of the sea with a neck spring, dressed for stormy weather, is a pottery pipe holder, 7". Post-Nippon mark of crossed arrows and 33/351 fired on base in black ink. $50.00 – 75.00.

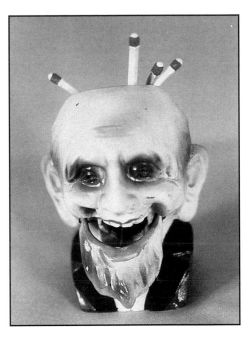

Plate 663. A toothless old man with a jaw wired like Breezy's, 3¾". He has a goatee and sparse outcropping of hair around his ears. His hollow head is intended for matches or toothpicks. Bisque porcelain. Pre-WWII Japan. $75.00.

Plate 661. A jolly fellow with his pipe in hand, 3¾". His head twirls on his long neck. Marked FOREIGN. $45.00 – 65.00.

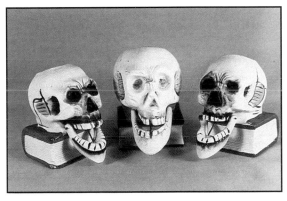

Plate 664. Hollow-eyed skull heads resting on a book of knowledge were souvenirs from Japan, copied from Ernst Böhne's nineteenth century porcelain skulls. They are found in several sizes and range from 2" to 4¼". Some are larger. Wired jaw movement. Rough edge of book pages is for a match striker and the hole on top of the head was for matches or toothpicks. Bisque with characteristic markings. Pre-WWII. $65.00 – 95.00 each.

Plate 662. H.M.S. Breezy, 4¼". An English sailor dressed in snappy blue and white uniform. The top of his hat is an ashtray. His lower jaw freely wags from an intricate wire and weight balance. "FOREIGN" on the bottom is a post-Nippon mark indicating Japanese wares for export. Bisque. $125.00.

Plate 665. Ashtrays with molded wings for yes nods. All are marked Patent T.T. and were found in New Zealand. $85.00 – 100.00 each.

Plate 666. More ashtrays from New Zealand. $85.00 – 100.00 each.

WEAR YOUR NODDER, WHY NOT?
Examples of nodders you can wear.

Plate 667. Wear a cat with a spring neck, or the happy rabbit with his carrot. What is more repulsive than biting into an apple with a worm in it? Biting into the apple with a half worm in it! Enameled pin of pot metal. $1.00 each.

Plate 668. Santa's whiskers wobble. Also streamers on the holiday wreath. From gift catalogs. 1980s. $65.00 each.

SOUVENIRS

Plate 669. Some lucky fellow received a "Best Husband Award," 5". Eyes behind black-rim glasses blink, flicker, that is, from motion of the coiled spring in his neck. Pottery painted head and glazed body. At one time probably had a paper sticker. The Vari-Vue Company of Mount Vernon, New York, held the patent on this moving animation. Circa 1950s. $23.00.

Plate 670. A "Souvenir of New Orleans, La." in the form of a black face cigarette ashpot, 2¼" x 3¾". A red tongue wags on wings in the open mouth. An amusing piece of bisque porcelain with Patent T.T. mark, pre-WWII Japan. $150.00 – 200.00.

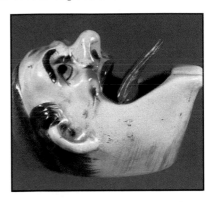

Plate 671 Another similar head ashpot souvenir with tongue wagging on wings, 2". Patent T.T. Japan. $150.00 – 200.00.

Plate 672. Bambi, pot metal and copper coated, 3½". Body crest is marked, Souvenir of Shasta Dam, California. Head nods on strip of spring steel. $65.00.

Plate 673. "Aloha," 6½". This hula gal has an anchor magnet under her feet. Painted pottery. She performs the hula from the spring in her hips. Japan. $25.00 – 35.00.

Plate 674. Just an animated strange collectible from Tarpon Springs, Florida. Circa 1982. Cost $1.99. $3.50.

Index

Bibliography

Aldridge, Eileen. *Porcelain*. New York:
  Gosset and Dunlap, 1970.

Angione, Genevieve. *All-Bisque and Half-Bisque Dolls*.
  Thomas Nelson & Sons, 1969.

Atterbury, Paul. *The History of Porcelain*. London:
  Orbis Publishing Limited, 1982.

Bainridge, Henry Charles. *Peter Carl Faberge*. London:
  B.T. Batsford Ltd., 1949.

Blackford, Bill and Martin Williams. *The Smithsonian Collection of Newspaper Comics*.
  Forward by Candady.

Blair, Ruth Van Ness. *Mary's Monster*. New York:
  Coward, McCann & Geoghegan, Inc. Junior Literary Guild selection, 1975.

Boger, Louise Ade. *The Dictionary of World Pottery and Porcelain*. New York:
  Charles Scribner's Sons, 1971.

Bond, Harold and Lewis Bond. *An Encyclopedia of Antiques*. New York:
  Tudor Publishing Co., 1947.

Brenner, Robert. *Christmas Revisited*. West Chester, PA:
  Schiffer Publishing Ltd., 1986.

Chu, Arthur and Grace. *Oriental Antiques and Collectibles, A Guide*. New York:
  Crown Publishers, Inc., 1973.

Cieslik, Jurgen and Marianne. *German Doll Encyclopedia 1800–1939*. Cumberland, MD:
  Hobby House Press, Inc., 1985.

Cole, Sheila. *The Dragon in the Cliff*. New York:
  Lathrop, Lee & Shepard, Juvenile Division, 1991.

Coleman, Dorothy S., Elizabeth A., and Evelyn J. *The Collector's Book of Dolls' Clothes*.
  New York: Crown Publishers, Inc., 1975.

Cox, Barry. *Prehistoric Animals*. New York:
  Grosset & Dunlap Publishers, 1970.

Cox, Warren E. *The Book of Pottery and Porcelain, Vol. I*. New York:
  Crown Publishers, Inc., 1944.

Culiff, Robert. *The World of Toys*. London – New York – Sydney – Toronto:
  The Hamlyn Publishing Group Limited, 1969.

Cushion, John P. *Pottery and Porcelain*. London:
  Chestergate House, Vauxhaill Bridge Road, 1970.

Danckert, Ludwig. *Dictionary of European Porcelain Marks, Makers, and Factories*.
  London: N.A.G. Press, 1981.

Donnelly, P.J. *Blanc de Chine, The Porcelain of Têhua in Fukien*. New York:
  Frederick A. Praeger Publishers, 1967.

Ducret, Siegfried. *German Porcelain and Faience*. New York:
  Universe Books, Inc., 1962.

Eberlein and Ramsdell. *The Practical Book of Chinaware*. Garden City, NY:
  Halcyon House, 1942.

Fisher, Stanley W. *Fine Porcelain and Pottery*. New York:
  Gallahad Books, 1975.

Foley, Dan. *Toys Through the Ages*. Philadelphia and New York:
    Chilton Books, 1962.

Hobson, R.L. *Chinese Pottery and Porcelain, Two Volumes*. New York:
    Dover Publications, Inc. 1976.

Honey, W.B. *Dresden China*. Albany, NY:
    Fort Orange Press, Ind., 1946.

Koch, Robert C. *Louis C. Tiffany's Glass, Bronzes*. New York:
    Crown Publishers, Inc., 1971.

Litchfield, Frederick. *Pottery and Porcelain, A Guide to Collectors*. New York:
    M. Barrows and Company, 1950.

Monteiro, George, *The Poetical Works of Longfellow*. Boston:
    Houghton Mifflin Company, 1975.

Paul, Tessa. *The Art of Louis Comfort Tiffany*. New York:
    Exter Books, 1987.

Phillips, John Goldsmith. *China–Trade Porcelain*. Cambridge, MA:
    Harvard University Press, 1956.

Ray, Marcia. *Collectible Ceramics*. New York:
    Crown Publishers, Inc., 1974.

Röntgen, Robert E. *Marks on German, Bohemian and Austrian Porcelain 1710 to the Present*. Exton, PA:
    Schiffer Publishing Ltd., 1981.

Röntgen, Robert E. *The Book of Meissen*. Exton, PA:
    Schiffer Publishing Ltd., 1984.

Schiffer, Herbert, Peter, and Nancy. *Chinese Export Porcelain*. Exton, PA:
    Schiffer Publishing Ltd., 1975.

Schoumatoff, Alex. *Russian Blood, A Family Chronicle*. New York:
    Vantage Books, A Division of Randon House, 1982.

Shull, Thelma. *Victorian Antiques*. Rutland, VT:
    Charles E. Tuttle Company, 1963.

Sonntag, Dr. Hans and Bettina Schuster. *Meissen. Europes Oldest Porcelain Manufactory*.
    Printed in Germany, 1991.

Springer, L. Elsinore. *The Collector's Book of Bells*. New York:
    Crown Publishers, Inc. 1972; Second Printing, March, 1979.

Van Ness, Ruth. *Mary's Monster, A Literary Guild Selection*.
    Coward, McCann & Geogehan, Inc., 1975.

Wilford, John Noble. *The Riddle of the Dinosaur*. New York:
    Alfred A. Knopf, 1985.

Encyclopedia of Antiques
Holy Bible, King James Version
Lexington Public Library
New York Public Library
The Encyclopedia Britannica
The Golden Glow©
University of Kentucky Library
World Book Encyclopedia